Praise for *Dearly Beloved*

"My dear sista Pamela Ayo Yetunde has written an evocative emergent journey that asks us to be with our beloved ancestor Prince Rogers Nelson, not simply read the words. Sista Pamela helps us see Prince through the prisms of Liberation, Care and Fugitivity. *Dearly Beloved* is a treaty of Love and the art of resisting being captured by others unimaginings. *Dearly Beloved* will invite you to your edges, and then ask if you're ready for more. This is truly a beautiful book and worthy of contemplation and appreciation."
Dr. Resmaa Menakem, *New York Times*–bestselling author of *My Grandmother's Hands*

"Ayo Yetunde and her new book on the deep meaning of Prince's eternal music are rare gifts that speak to our heart and our soul, that inspire us to reimagine the power of song, soul, and creativity in facing the awe and the ache that lives in us and around us in troubled times. Poetic and profound, this is a book that should be savored and used for contemplating how this artist and art make us whole."
Doug Abrams, coauthor of *The Book of Joy*

"Pamela Ayo Yetunde invites you to journey with Prince to the place of beloved awakening: a place where you are beloved not because you are worthy, but simply because you are. Being beloved is grace. If you know this, *Dearly*

Beloved will embrace you. If you don't know this, *Dearly Beloved* will shatter you, and then awaken you. In either case, this is a book worthy of your time and attention."
 Rabbi Rami Shapiro, author of *Perennial Wisdom for the Spiritually Independent*

"Pamela Ayo Yetunde brings the wealth of Christian as well as Buddhist traditions to bear in this book, and spells out in detail the spiritual and theological themes embedded in the music of iconic artist Prince, masterfully conveying the message to every reader, that you are, indeed, in a cosmic and existential kind of way, Dearly Beloved!"
 Ruben L. F. Habito, author of *Healing Breath: Zen for Christians and Buddhists in a Wounded World*, *Be Still and Know: Zen and the Bible*, and others

"*Dearly Beloved* is a deeply resonant work for those of us who discovered the sacred on the dance floor, with Prince's music as our guide. As someone who found both sexual awakening and divine connection through Prince's rhythms, this book speaks to the heart of what it means to experience God in unexpected places. Yetunde captures the essence of Prince's spirituality—his unapologetic embrace of the erotic, the spiritual, and the socially conscious—and weaves it into a narrative that is both deeply personal and universally relevant. *Dearly Beloved* is an essential read for anyone who, like me, has danced their way to God, and for those guiding others in spiritual formation. It is a reminder that the sacred is not confined to the traditional but is alive

in the pulse of a bassline, the sway of hips, and the freedom to be fully oneself in the presence of the divine."
Rev. Tandi Rogers, Director of Spiritual Direction Formation & Certification at Meadville Lombard Theological School

"In *Dearly Beloved*, Ayo Yetunde takes us on a multisensory excursion examining the life and spiritual exploration of the musician Prince. He was an enormous talent, expressing privately through his life, but publicly through his songs and performances, his deep longing for creation and connection, both with his listeners and later with the divine. From the theosophical perspective, we struggle to transform the merely sensory into the ineffable and lasting, and his life reflected this, perhaps more visibly than most."
Douglas Keene, President of The Theosophical Society in America

"This book is something remarkable—more than yet another posthumous blessing of a singular musical talent but a brilliant reframing of Prince as theologian. His entire canon, B-sides and all, is mined and clarified not only so we can understand his complex faith, but better understand our own. An important contribution to music and church!"
Rev. Julian "J.Kwest" DeShazier, pastor and artist

"Transformed people transform people. Dr. Yetunde makes the compelling case for the transformation of Prince from a place of religious trauma to a mystical prophet for the people. The invitation is here in depth for all of us to listen and groove with Prince and his many collaborators to become a part of the Dearly Beloved Community. Prince changed the world and Dr. Yetunde tells us how and why in this beautiful work."

Rev. T. Michael Rock, Director of Contextual Education and Spiritual Direction at United Theological Seminary of the Twin Cities

"In Dearly Beloved, we are invited to see Prince not just as an artist but as a modern-day theologian who, like the Apostle Paul, wrestled with the complexities of faith, freedom, and identity. This work beautifully positions Prince's body of work within the cannon of liberation theology, offering us a profound understanding of his spiritual journey and the liberatory power of his preached gospel. This book is a testament to the idea that we are all 'fearfully and wonderfully made' (Psalm 139:14). A *must-read* for those seeking to deepen their understanding of the divine through music, media, and the beauty of the 'everyday things we do.'"

Teddy raShaan, PhD, Curator of Religion, Smithsonian National Museum of African American History & Culture

"Ever since the deeply sensual love poem known as the Song of Songs was included in the Bible, eroticism and mysticism have had a lasting connection. Prince, who created music as transcendent and spiritual as it is unabashedly sexy, stands in that deliciously integral tradition. Now Ayo Yetunde playfully and insightfully unpacks both the contradictions and the epiphanies encoded in Prince's work. *Dearly Beloved* charts a remarkable spiritual journey, and invites us to find our own sacred path therein."

Carl McColman, author of *Eternal Heart* and *Read the Bible Like a Mystic*

"Whether you share the author's interpretations of Prince's spirituality or bring your own perspective, *Dearly Beloved* is more than a book examining Prince's spiritual journey— it's an invitation and practical guide to exploring and deepening your own. Through "up(ward)" listening and viewing practices of Prince's songs and films, this book empowers you to embrace the truth that you are beloved and dear by encouraging you to reflect on and question your spiritual inheritances and history."

De Angela L. Duff, educator, Associate Vice Provost at New York University (NYU), curator of Prince symposia, and creator of *What Did Prince Do This Week?*

"This rigorous and inspiring text makes a compelling case for why we would do well to engage Prince as a prophetic witness in these times. Framed around his core idea that we are all "dearly beloved" Ayo's close reading reveals an artist whose resistance to narrow binaries, and objectifying ways of thinking and being invites us to not only "get through

this thing called life," but to accept our own and each others vulnerabilities with humility and love."
> **Lisa Anderson,** Director of Leadership, Auburn Theological Seminary

"In *Dearly Beloved,* Ayo Yetunde brings us closer to the heart of Prince's music. Beneath the vitality of his vast collection, there is a search for meaning, deeper connection, and liberation. While his music is dazzling, we can see ourselves reflected in his longing for acceptance just as we are and fully human with original goodness. This is a book that you feel and savor the moments of inspiration."
> **Cheryl A. Giles**, Senior Lecturer Emerita, Harvard Divinity School

"In this singularly compelling book, Ayo Yetunde channels the many complex facets of Prince through the prism of his theologies, revealing the previously unexplored spiritual insights and perspectives of this great artist. This invaluable work will be a boon to any Prince admirer wanting to learn more about his focus on spiritual healing."
> **Rev. SeiFu Anil Singh-Molares**, Executive Director, Spiritual Directors International

Dearly Beloved

DEARLY BELOVED

PRINCE, SPIRITUALITY, & THIS THING CALLED LIFE

PAMELA AYO YETUNDE

Broadleaf Books
Minneapolis

DEARLY BELOVED
Prince, Spirituality, and This Thing Called Life

Copyright © 2025 Pamela Ayo Yetunde. Published by Broadleaf Books. All rights reserved. Except for brief quotations in critical articles or reviews, no part of this book may be reproduced in any manner without prior written permission from the publisher. Email copyright@broadleafbooks.com or write to Permissions, Broadleaf Books, PO Box 1209, Minneapolis, MN 55440-1209.

29 28 27 26 25 24   1 2 3 4 5 6 7 8 9

Library of Congress Cataloging-in-Publication Data

Names: Yetunde, Pamela Ayo, author.
Title: Dearly beloved : Prince, spirituality, and this thing called life / Pamela Ayo Yetunde.
Description: Minneapolis : Broadleaf Books, 2025. | Includes bibliographical references. |
Identifiers: LCCN 2024033564 (print) | LCCN 2024033565 (ebook) | ISBN 9798889831600 (hardcover) | ISBN 9798889831617 (ebook)
Subjects: LCSH: Prince—Criticism and interpretation. | Prince—Religion. | Sex in music. | Rock music—History and criticism. | Rock music—Religious aspects.
Classification: LCC ML420.P974 Y47 2025 (print) | LCC ML420. P974 (ebook) | DDC 781.66092—dc23/eng/20240723
LC record available at https://lccn.loc.gov/2024033564
LC ebook record available at https://lccn.loc.gov/2024033565

Cover design: © 2024 Gabe Nansen
Cover image: Prince © 2024 Shutterstock; digital flow/349942286 by Photobank.kiev.ua

Print ISBN: 979-8-8898-3160-0
eBook ISBN: 979-8-8898-3161-7

Printed in China

To the Indianapolis, Indiana, radio station WTLC and all the DJs who dared to play Prince in the late 1970s and 1980s when it was morally risky to do so.

To all the DJs who play contemporary gospel music today who are courageous enough to give Prince's body of work serious theological consideration and provide precious airtime for his music to be heard for the gospel that it is.

Table of Contents

Preface   ix

Introduction   1

1. Dearly Beloved
   I Want to Be Your Lover   21
2. We Are Gathered   61
3. Here Today
   (But . . . You Have to Wake Up and Cross That Graffiti Bridge)   83
4. To Get Through This Thing   115
5. Called Life   131
6. Evil, Temptation, the Afterworld, and Going Crazy   147
7. Redemption and the Rising of the Rainbow Children   179
8. Conclusion   197

Epilogue
This Is What It Feels Like When Doves Cry   211
Afterword   233

Acknowledgments   241
Notes   245

Preface

> **Listen Along**
>
> Welcome 2 America
>
> *If you don't know who Prince was, please watch the concert film* Sign O' The Times, *then proceed to read this book. I recommend you also listen to "Welcome 2 America." At the beginning of each chapter, I recommend a list of Prince's songs I think you would do well to listen to before reading the chapter because the music will provide the artistic context for the words I've written and the spiritual practices I'm recommending.*

I am a pastoral counselor raised in the United Methodist Church. From as early as I can remember until I was eighteen years old, I went to church weekly, engaged in prayer, recited the Nicene Creed, knelt at the altar monthly for communion, engaged in service projects, led our youth group, and was taught that the Bible was the inerrant (to be taken literally) word of God. Like countless trillions of Christians throughout history, I was conditioned to believe sex for pleasure, not pro-creation, and outside marriage was an eternally damnable sin. I never questioned this belief system nor did anyone in my small circle—save my first boyfriend—try to wrestle the belief from me. I kept my legs closed as my mother taught me to do.

Virginal purity, in hindsight, was a privilege I didn't understand as a privilege until I saw a couple of girlfriends removed from school because they became unwed pregnant teenagers. One family moved out of the neighborhood because their youngest teenage daughter was pregnant. Rumor had it she was impregnated by their neighbor. In the mid-1970s in the Midwest, if you were a girl in "the church" who wanted sexual and reproductive freedom, you ran the risk of being labeled as "fast," as in, sexually precocious, or a "hussy," a girl who was not really sexually free but sexually sick and morally deviant. So, a lot was riding on my virginal purity, but that "lot"—that privilege—was reevaluated as I began to listen to Prince.

If Prince's music could penetrate the Christian mores of my upbringing in the '70s, '80s, and beyond, is it possible his music still has that influence and power?

WARNING: This book is not for grown folks who want or need to hold fast to their piety. This book is for grown folks who are open-minded and open-hearted for a body of artistic work dedicated to helping Prince art consumers resolve, simply put, the tensions between good and bad, God and Satan, intrapsychically and socially, politically and spiritually. The resolution of these tensions cannot be found in capitalistic industrial nations such as the United States. Therefore, in his song "Welcome 2 America," Prince sings about how the glitter and glam of the United States is an illusion. In America, it sometimes seems as though everyone is wealthy when in fact the illusion is built on the backs of the oppressed and the transformation that needs to take place is really within ourselves.

Welcome to Prince as a spiritual guide for this thing called life. Please note: this book is rated "E" for being explicitly sexual and explicitly spiritual.

Prince identified with evangelical traditions I am not a part of. The purpose of this book is not to convert, evangelize, missionize, or proselytize readers to a religion. Prince and I were part of Christian traditions, with religious resources, that are informed by antisemitic, anti-Catholic, anti-paganist, anti-universalist, and anti-spiritualist thought. I have worked to disentangle myself from hatred, and it remains a work in progress because culture sometimes holds a mirror to teachings I received long before I knew the prejudices associated with those teachings. For purposes of this book, I have chosen not to overly indulge the hatred embedded in our shared and inherited theologies, which arguably, there's hardly an explicit trace of it in Prince's early art. I believe his art, taken as a whole, may support us in getting through this thing called life without becoming agents of destruction.

How? By appreciating art itself. As a consequence of reflecting on Prince's art again as I worked on this manuscript, his art inspired me to write a poem that I have included in the epilogue. On one hand, as Prince may have said, "It'll all come out in the wash." On the other hand, as you read about Prince's art and experience images, feelings, and your own creative impulses, you may not be able to wait until it all comes out in the wash. While you read this book, I invite you to use a journal to write your own poetic verses, lyrics, and commentaries so that by the time you finish reading, you will see your inner self reflected in the "wash" of your journal entries.

Introduction

Listen Along

Bambi
Graffiti Bridge
Housequake
The Cross
When Doves Cry

Prince Rogers Nelson (June 7, 1958–April 21, 2016), the music legend who went by the singular name Prince, and for a time also went by the moniker "The Artist Formerly Known as Prince," was an extraordinary multi-instrumentalist musician and artist who left a treasure trove of recorded and unrecorded music. Before he died, he released more than forty albums and hundreds of singles, many of which were mega hits between 1978 and 1993 and are still being played four decades later. Prince's music is irrefutably classic. It is no wonder why he was admitted into the Rock and Roll Hall of Fame in 2004. I argue he should be admitted into the Gospel Hall of Fame, but I'll make my case about that later.

I was in high school in politically and morally conservative and racially divided Indianapolis, Indiana, when Prince released his first album, *For You*. I had been raised in the United Methodist Church, where every Sunday we sang hymn after hymn. I say that to say, my consciousness was developed to have an aversion toward bold sexual expressions, so I didn't really hear it even when it was right in my ears because it wasn't yet in my consciousness. I discovered Prince's music on Indianapolis's Black radio station, WTLC. The AM radio stations where I listened to pop, rock, and southern rock were the only radio stations available on our car radio, and the DJs were not playing Prince. I thought it was because the rhythm was considered R&B and therefore Black, but perhaps his initial absence from pop stations was not about race and culture. After all, you could hear Michael Jackson and The Commodores (featuring Lionel Richie), but I don't remember hearing Prince on AM radio early in his career. The first song I remember hearing on WTLC was the bouncy "Soft and Wet." It is about painful coitus, but he uses the word "sugarcane" to describe the penis. I had no idea what he was singing about because I knew nothing about double entendre. But my body loved to dance to the music I heard and I allowed my body to swerve, bop, and dance as if it was a G-rated song, which in hindsight, it obviously was not!

"Dig, if you will, a picture . . ." as Prince put it in "When Doves Cry." I couldn't dig it because I couldn't decode it. I didn't even know there was a code: I was only sixteen or seventeen years old and a Christian virgin. At that time, many girls that age were virgins, or pretending to be. This was 1978, and a backlash to the hippy free-sex movement was afoot. It was a time when it was so shameful to be a pregnant teenager that it was deemed culturally appropriate to be removed from your school to avoid shame on your family and encouragement to other girls to have premarital sex.

The following year, I was living in a college dorm and my next-door neighbor, a white girl (a woman-child really) and professed evangelical Christian, who I'll call Debbie, had a Prince poster hanging on her wall. He was bare-chested and wearing a thong. This was 1980. I may not have known what "Soft and Wet" meant when I first heard it, but by the time I got to college, I knew it was risqué for a white evangelical Christian woman, grown or not, to have a scantily clad Black man on a poster in her room. By Christian and white standards of the day, my friend Debbie knew it was an act of defiance, a coming-of-age decision, to have that Prince poster prominently displayed on her wall, but it so endeared me to her.

Thanks to Debbie's Prince poster, I began to believe that together we could cross cultural bridges and become friends—and we did indeed become close friends. Our shared love of Prince led me to examine some of my own biases against and stereotypes about white people. For example, it was said that white people were rhythmically challenged, but watching Debbie dance to Prince would have proved wrong all the white racial stereotypes about them being unable to dance with funk. In fact, her ability to dance to Prince gave me permission to loosen up from a Christian Black respectability and dance without abandon and love Prince in a way I had not before and also in a way I didn't fully understand at the time. I was shaking loose the fear of being morally deviant, the fear of not being viewed as respectable by conservative Christian Black standards of the time, and the fear of God's wrath.

Prince's music was part of the soundtrack of my developmental process into adulthood, especially while I was in college between 1980 and 1984—a time fraught with the rise of a new kind of pent-up sexual Puritanism that Prince and his group, The Revolution, unabashedly railed against. His art was alluring and arresting. I was a young woman living unsupervised on a college campus, which meant I could do most anything without my puritanical mother knowing. In a way, this was frightening because I grew up in the United Methodist Church and internalized what I was taught—sex outside marriage was a damnable sin. Who was right: my church, me and Debbie, or Prince?

Despite his overarching image of being a sex machine, Prince's music carries serious spiritual significance. In fact, I'd argue he represents a unique class of music that I'll call "funk-rock gospel"—a thorough mix of raunchy and righteous. If you allow yourself to feel both impulses inside of you, you'll know better the reason why Prince was a singular sensation—he created and performed art to speak to both aspects of the human condition throughout his recording career, seeking to reconcile the desire for sexual engagement and pleasure on one side and Seventh-day Adventist piety on the other side.

Take a moment and listen to his guitar licks on "Bambi." It is the kind of sound that makes you want to play an air guitar and rock your whole body forward and backward like you're a heavy metal rock star. Or what about the drum beats at the beginning of "Housequake"? The rhythm, if you allow it, concentrates in your pelvic area; moving your hips is about the only natural thing to do. The bouncy rhythms of "I Would Die 4 U" are hypnotic from the start. In the chant, Prince seems to channel Jesus Christ himself—as if calling one of his lost sheep sings "you" and repeats the word in case the listener doesn't think Prince is singing to them "you, I would die for you." With that hypnotic sound, channeling Jesus, and singing to his Dearly Beloveds, we get a better picture of what it feels like to be delivered from conservative and conventional ways of responding to music—from the vantage point of an observer or consumer to an embodied participant in liberation. This is the power of Prince's desire to be humanity's lover.

This is why I proclaim Prince was a funk-rock gospel artist and reigns as king of the international funk-rock gospel empire. I contend his 1990 movie, *Graffiti Bridge*, is a gospel movie that should be viewed through the eyes of love and wisdom, but it was panned for obvious reasons: poor acting (save Morris Day), poor direction, a weak script, and many compositions that fell beneath Prince's proven brilliance. Nevertheless, *Graffiti Bridge* is arguably Prince's crowning glory of an artistic expression of his belief that sexuality and spirituality are one. I believe the founders of tantric sex and the *Kama Sutra* would agree.

    Nearly forty years after Prince's first album was released and a year after his death, I moved to St. Paul, Minnesota—the "twin city" of Prince's place of birth and home, Minneapolis. I had moved from Atlanta (Hotlanta) to teach in "Minnesnowda" at a Christian seminary affiliated with the United Church of Christ, United Theological Seminary of the Twin Cities. Yes, I was a Buddhist practitioner and lay leader (how I "converted" to Buddhism is an entirely different story) hired as a full-time faculty member at a liberal Christian seminary, in part, because I was also skilled in interreligious immersion and spiritual care. I was hired to teach spiritual care and pastoral counseling and lead the burgeoning interreligious chaplaincy program where I introduced the idea of the Theology of Prince project; we took students to Paisley Park, issued a call for submissions to our *Theology of Prince Journal*, presented in the University of Minnesota's "Prince from Minneapolis" symposium in 2018, and of course, hosted a dance party and poetry slam at the seminary. Despite Prince's sexuality evangelism, I thought a Minnesota Christian seminary should focus on Prince as a theologian-musician.

Although Prince did not attend college, divinity school, or seminary, Prince was a Christian theologian. A theologian, simply put, is someone who studies the nature of God and gods and those who think about God and gods. Prince was a student of many religious traditions throughout his life and applied his studies in his lyrics and music, but he was a Christian heavily influenced by Seventh-day Adventism, the *Kama Sutra*, and, later in life, Jehovah's Witness theologies. I argue that at some point in his life between his upbringing and his baptism in the Jehovah's Witness religion, he was actually a "Theosophist Christian," someone who believed in the divinity of Jesus. He also incorporated teachings from other religions into his worldview. In his song "Family Name," he begins by welcoming listeners to the "Akashic Records Genetic Information Division." The Akashic records are, according to my understanding, a material but invisible system of categorization of all historical events. The Akashic record belief is part of Theosophy, but that doesn't mean Prince identified as a Theosophist. According to the Theosophical Society in America (TSA) archivist Janet Kerschner, Prince was never a member of the TSA and never made a formal research request. Nevertheless, throughout Prince's career, he incorporated religious, spiritual, and theological thoughts and concepts in his music, album cover art, and *Graffiti Bridge* trilogy.

His parents were influenced by Seventh-day Adventism, a Christian reformist tradition, and Prince grew up in reformist traditions, embraced another reforming tradition, and lived his life in a reforming conformity spirit. No one

I know, however, has ever called him a gospel artist or a theologian. Yet, upon close examination of his music through Seventh-day Adventists and Jehovah's Witnesses theological lenses, even through the lenses of mainline Protestant thought and the *Kama Sutra*, I conclude that Prince was indeed a theologian who used his music, movies, and videos to witness and proclaim his sexuality-reformist, Seventh-day Adventist, interreligious-theosophist, and then conversely conventionally sexually conservative Jehovah's Witnesses' theologies. Why is this important to understand? Freedom of conscience is a core value in Prince's belief system. Freedom of conscience supports happiness and wholeness. Wholeness is experienced when we can examine ourselves, accept ourselves as we authentically are, and work toward the reconciliation of diametrically opposing values within our psyches, even when those opposing values are from opposing belief systems. Happiness and wholeness can be fruits of the freedom of conscience because the exercise of this freedom can lead to love.

This is a book of spiritual practices inspired by Prince's art. As a pastoral counselor, a chaplain, a spiritual director, a spiritual companion, a practical pastoral theologian, a Buddhologist, and an activist and advocate (I've been called many things), I think it is of great importance to amplify Prince's spiritual message abstracted from the mesmerizing music that, in one way, has obscured his central theological messages. In another way, the music has helped some of us feel his message in our bones. This abstraction is of critical importance to me because what Prince called the *apocalyptic*

Armageddon, which we might now call *climate catastrophe*, is here, has been here, is increasingly encroaching on and eroding our ways of life, and it appears as if we are living like powerless victims destined for destruction, even self-destruction and genocide. Why be stuck in victimhood when we can at least dance, have sex, or go nuts?

Prince's lyrics provide joyful and realistic encouragement irrespective of whether we agree with his religious beliefs. I wonder about the impact of his physical absence on this earth. He sang, "I Would Die 4 U." One could argue that he certainly lived for us, so how might we make his untimely death from an accidental fentanyl drug overdose mean something to someone else? Can we, his fans, help carry the narrative and artifacts of his life and uplift others? We're already doing it. How can we make his body of work more poignant for our pop lives right now? I truly believe we can use Prince's music dialectically (arguably his artist life's ambition) for psycho-spiritual healing. We are a species that lives with the experience of being internally divided against ourselves and externally divided against others. It is little wonder why we are in the climate predicament we are facing. Prince's emphasis on being gathered was a practice of unifying those pitted against others on ridiculous grounds, including the ridiculousness of unnecessary conflicts based on race, gender, nationality, religion, sexuality, and so on. Prince & The Revolution symbolized inclusivity.

Prince, in his art, revealed a way of understanding the Seventh-day Adventist foundational theology of The Great Controversy as written about by Ellen G. White in her book of the same title, originally published in 1858. What is The Great Controversy? It is, according to some Seventh-day Adventist theology, the irreconcilability (by human beings) of diametrically opposing consequential phenomena—God and Satan, life and death, right and wrong, sin and sinlessness. The concept of The Great Controversy is thousands of years old and describes a battle in which Satan attempts to overthrow God and deceive human beings, making humans follow ungodly laws. No human being can ever resolve these great controversies, but God can and will when Judgment Day comes. Before that day comes, when it comes, there will be opportunities for repentance and redemption. In the meantime, there will be signs that the resolution of The Great Controversy (or controversies) is coming. The goal is to be completely faithful to God while simultaneously resisting Satan's temptation. Prince's album *Controversy* is a testament to this realization and revelation. He was concerned with questions of ultimacy, as in, what is true and right above all things we believe to be true and right. What is the final source or who is the first creator of the final say? Where does the buck stop? Who or what can I really trust? These are ultimacy concerns and questions.

In addition to overarching ultimacy concerns and questions, Prince was concerned about sex. Is sex ultimately wrong if the only way people are born is through sex? Is sex ultimately wrong because it can be pleasurable? Is pleasure wrong if the sensation was created by God, and God is ultimately good, so what God creates is ultimately good, including pleasure and pleasure derived from sex, which may lead to birth? For Prince, sexual pleasure only had divine purpose. That is, until the rise of AIDS, the deformation and death of his child, and a retreat to religious fundamentalism, which changed Prince's beliefs, perspectives, mission, and art. The reality of a communicable disease spread by sexual contact changed Prince's gospel (if you will) of sexual pleasure. Love emerged. Prince used the archetypes of the winged white horse, the ankh, and water to express his propheticism and his use of archetypes helped cultivate the mythology of Prince as a messiah, but was it just a myth? Was he the messiah of kink, both blasphemous and liberatory?

Ultimate concerns and questions can arise when one is confronted with opposing truths. For example, if the Christian God gave his only son to save people from sin and destroys everyone else, is God good or bad? Is there only black or white? Male or female? Up or down? Front or back, left or right? These words with the word "or" in between are examples of poles, as in polarized—divided into only two opposing realities—like The Great Controversy. Is the thing, person, or experience good or is it bad? Of God or of Satan? Prince wanted to know if sex was good or bad and if sexual pleasure was good or bad, of God or Satan. He was on the path to ultimacy about these polarities and eventually theologically worked out a nonpolarized, nondual understanding of sexuality, but may have reversed himself again near the end of his life in the name of theology.

There is much in Prince's music and movies to psychoanalyze. The purpose of this book is not psychoanalysis per se but to understand Prince's journey toward nonduality and his body of work toward a nondual consciousness. The journey toward nonduality was a quest for psychological and spiritual healing and something he offered his fans through his music. In his song "Family Name," he writes about race and that the terms Black and white are a delusion. Ultimately, these words represent the concept of "this or that"—"this" being true and "that" being what counters truth—finding the truth, through dialecticism, can be found in the cosmic fabric of our existence once our minds are free of delusion.

***

We are being invited to look at the high-minded moralist and the primitive in Prince and in each of us. Why? To cultivate wholeness, well-being, and the inner peace of the Paisley Park people.

Much of Prince's art is misunderstood. The purpose of this book is to "exegete" his music for comfort and resilience in troubling times. Exegete? That's a fancy word typically used by theologians who are analyzing sacred texts or works by "legitimated" theologians. So, for those who think Prince (who did not go to college, divinity school, or seminary) is not a legitimate theologian worthy of an exegesis, please take into consideration that not everyone is recognized for who they are when they are alive. The University of Minnesota, also in 2018, posthumously conferred an honorary doctorate of humane letters degree to Prince. I would like to see some divinity schools and seminaries do the same. Moreover,

I have a dare, maybe even a double-dare, for gospel music artists, but I'll say more about that in the conclusion.

Prince worked with brilliant musicians including Wendy Melvoin and Lisa Coleman, members of Prince & The Revolution. Melvoin said that while they were composing the *Purple Rain* album:

> [Prince] was still kneeling and praying to God, and he really believed in signs and certain things he was trying and then waking up going, "I know this and that!" calling us in the middle of the night going, "I've seen it! I know it—it's appeared!" He was so much more fearless about figuring it out. Now he's studied scripture, but when he was younger, he wasn't spouting scriptures and parables. It was just an abstract thing.

And Coleman said

> Prince was writing songs that were not confused, but searching. He wasn't limiting himself by his religion; he was allowing it to fuel his work.

How was Prince's religion fueling his sexual expression?

One of the songs on the *Purple Rain* album (the version that is rated "E") is "We Can Fuck." In this song written with The Revolution, they reference the *Kama* (pleasure) *Sutra*, an ancient Indian text on sex, society, and religion.

Prince alludes to the fact that the *Kama Sutra* is wordy, and in his sexual prowess, can excite his lover with only half the words or really half the moves the *Kama Sutra* offers.

I mention the *Kama Sutra* in the introduction because I believe its influence on Prince's music lasted throughout his recording career and informed his music as well as the *Graffiti Bridge* movie and helps explain how his sexuality, his religions, and the Seventh-day Adventist concept of The Great Controversy informed his art.

This book is inspired by and largely organized by the opening lines in Prince's song "Let's Go Crazy" on the *Purple Rain* album, which he recorded with his band Prince & The Revolution: "Dearly beloved, we are gathered here today, to get through this thing called life . . ." The Prince, Prince & The Revolution, Prince & The New Power Generation, and Prince & 3rdeyegirl playlist for this book include references to these songs:

$
7
1999
affirmation I & II
affirmation III
Alphabet St.
America
Anna Stesia
Annie Christian
Art Official Cage
Automatic

Baltimore
Bambi
Boom
Can't Stop This Feeling I Got
Christopher Tracy's Parade
Colonized Mind
Condition of the Heart
Darling Nikki
Delirious
Diamonds and Pearls
Do it All Night
Do U Lie?
D.M.S.R.
Dreamer
Elephants & Flowers
Eye No
Family Name
Forever in My Life
Free
Gett Off
Graffiti Bridge
Head
Housequake
If I Was Your Girlfriend
International Lover
I Wanna Be Your Lover
I Would Die 4 U
Joy in Repetition
Lady Cab Driver

Little Red Corvette
Love Machine
Lovesexy
Melody Cool
Muse 2 the Pharaoh
New Power Generation
New Power Generation, Pt. 2
New World
One of Us
Paisley Park
Play in the Sunshine
Pop Life
Positivity
Private Joy
Purple Rain
Release It
Revelation
Ronnie, Talk to Russia
Round and Round
Sex in the Summer
Sexuality
Shake!
Sister
Sometimes It Snows in April
Still Would Stand All Time
Strange Relationship
Tambourine
Temptation
The Ballad of Dorothy Parker

The Cross
The Holy River
The Ladder
The Latest Fashion
The Love We Make
The Rainbow Children
The Question of U
Thieves in the Temple
Tick, Tick, Bang
We Can Fuck
We Can Funk
Welcome 2 America
When Doves Cry
When 2 R in Love

These eighty-three songs are just a fraction of Prince's recorded songs as an individual artist or with The Revolution, New Power Generation, or 3rdEyeGirl.

Prince's movie, *Graffiti Bridge*, is so coded that it begs for decoding. I offer what I can to that enterprise, knowing that using only a fraction of his work will produce a fraction of understanding and material for meaning-making. Please forgive me in advance if I have not included your favorite songs, albums, and movies in this book.

The art I have included is meant to help us feel into our innate goodness so that being Dearly Beloved is not just a concept but a belief that we come to know there is value in intentionally gathering with others for beneficial purposes; there are ethical obligations when we are gathered; we understand there are opportunities and responsibilities in being here today; we should remember our being here today comes with the reality that our next moment of existence is not guaranteed; and we use the word "life" to describe the dynamics of our existence, but one word can't capture it and describe it, so we learn to be in the mystery of life and what we know life to be. Prince was concerned, maybe obsessed, with evil and temptation, so he wanted to deeply understand it, let his fans know of his thinking, create art to inform and inspire, and later in life, share teachings from his religious community of Jehovah's Witnesses. He was steadfast on this mission and even though I do not share Prince's belief systems in their entirety, I do believe there are things we can do to create a more heavenly existence on earth because we are here today.

As a pastoral counselor interested in spiritual practices that help us cultivate resiliency in this thing we call life, I let Prince's lyrics inspire me to craft spiritual practices for you. In this book, you will find more than thirty practices for improving self-awareness, reducing the power of prejudices, improving your ability to experience internal and external harmony, valuing and exercising freedom, cultivating a healthy sexuality and lifestyle, and of course, love.

On the question of sex, I have my own beliefs coming out of the body of a woman who was a girl growing up in the 1960s, '70s, and '80s (I was a late bloomer) in the Midwest in a United Methodist church and household. I have traveled quite a distance from my religious and social upbringing and have done some of my own nondual work about what it means to be male or female. On one hand, nothing in this book about Prince's sexual art should be taken to suggest I agree or don't agree with it. On the other hand, I will say that nonconsensual sex can lead to lifelong trauma and should be renounced by the would-be aggressor. Sex with a minor cannot be consensual because a minor's prefrontal cortex is not fully developed and because they haven't grown in wisdom; the would-be aggressor should avoid sexual touch with a minor. Prince's song "Sister" is disgusting and wrong and should not be used as justification for incest and sex with a minor. I highly respect Prince's body of work, but I don't think his legacy is 100 percent pristine—it most certainly is not.

I end this book with a poem I dedicate to Prince because as I deeply reflected on his life and work, the process inspired me to express myself spontaneously through verse. Funny, but often in Buddhist texts, when someone experiences an awakening after hearing the Buddha, they recite their experience in verse before they go to heaven or experience nirvana. Is Prince a Buddha for me?

My hope is that this book will help you know with conviction that you are Dearly Beloved, appreciate the beauty of life and its vicissitudes through Prince's lyrics, and embrace wholesome ways to meet its challenges while keeping your self-dignity and compassion for others intact—the sounds of doves crying are getting louder every day.

1
Dearly Beloved

I Want to Be Your Lover

Listen Along

7
1999
Annie Christian
Christopher Tracy's Parade
Diamonds and Pearls
Do U Lie?
Family Name
If I Was Your Girlfriend
I Wanna Be Your Lover
I Would Die 4 U

> Joy in Repetition
> Little Red Corvette
> Private Joy
> Purple Rain
> Raspberry Beret
> Sometimes It Snows in April
> Strange Relationship
> Tamborine
> The Ballad of Dorothy Parker
> Thieves in the Temple

Dearly Beloved . . .
    Stop. Wait for it. Did you feel it?
I apologize for the interruption. You were just invited into a feeling of unconditional and tender positive regard (borrowing language from the psychologist Carl Rogers), an acknowledgment of your preciousness. *Dearly Beloved*, did you just blow through the experience of being addressed as your purest and most innate goodness in the habituated way we've all been taught to read, anticipating the next word, then the next, then the next until we get to the end of the sentence to make meaning of a sentence, a paragraph, a page, a chapter, then the entire book? Or, did you stop to ponder the salutation *"Dearly Beloved"*? Let's try it again.
Dearly Beloved . . .
    This time, did you try the words on for size? Did you embrace being called by the tender vulnerableness deep inside yourself? Or, after trying these words on, did you

reject the sweetness of yourself based on past harms you may have committed or a sense that you are flawed at your core? Please pause and take a moment to reflect and then return to the words "dearly" and "beloved." Allow the feelings to sink in. As you do, whether you know Prince's music or not (please remember to watch *Sign O' The Times*), you will get the sense of how his unconditional positive regard for others was felt and why his fans loved him with a mad passion, even if they felt they were doing wrong.

Dearly Beloved. As I reflect on these words, even if only saying them aloud to myself, I feel tender and vulnerable, supple and fragile like a baby. As I stay with the feeling, I also feel protective, even though no external threat is present. What am I protecting myself from? That aspect of consciousness that works toward convincing me that I am not dear or a beloved is called the "internal saboteur" in a psychological theory called Object Relations Theory. W. R. D. Fairbairn coined the term, which also means "the anti-libidinal ego" or "the harsh inner critic." In short, multiple egos form under infant stress. Depending on how intensely the stress impacts ego formation, an internal and unconscious world is created whereby feelings of love are attacked by the internal saboteur. The internal saboteur attacks the energy of love. I'll get into more detail about this intrapsychic dynamic in chapter two. It suffices to say for now that it's not always easy to respond positively to being called beloved nor is it easy to feel this way about others without conditions. For many, their insecurities arise when they are actively relating to those who have shamed or abused them. I resonate with Prince's equivalent of the internal saboteur that he called "Spooky Electric." In "Positivity," he wrote that Spooky Electric is that part of ourselves that is so doubtful about ourselves, it hurts to the core, can overtake our confidence and self-worth, and confuse us about our higher nature. He also used the term Spooky Electric to describe evil and Satan.

Even if we harbor thoughts about our innate goodness, feel discouraged, and become a victim, we are still beloved, in part, because we can choose to positively orient our hearts and minds. "This thing called life," as Prince put it, is exhausting and sometimes excruciating, so to have a talented musician call his fans "Dearly Beloved" is like a salve, wrapped in a beat and melody that can serve (momentarily and especially if the music is hypnotic) to help us remember we are worthy of being seen, heard, understood, respected, loved, healed from past injuries, and protected from future harm. For Prince, that meant to live in paradise forever, on earth.

Prince as a Symbol

We can use any number of paradoxical metaphors to describe Prince: the preacher in the boudoir, the savior in the dens of iniquity, the messiah in the brothel, the *Kama Sutra* priest, the light bearer in darkness, a cartographer for the lost, the Spiritual Trickster. No matter how we describe him, he wanted to lead us to the Purple Rain, a transcendent baptism-like experience where sadness, fear, jealousy, rage, character flaws, and insecurity are washed away. It is a conversion experience where extraordinary extroversion (a concept I discuss in detail in the next chapter) can be experienced and where libidinal energy can gain power to disempower Spooky Electric.

From a pastoral counselor's perspective, having counseled many people in a variety of settings regarding their inner conflicts between "right" and "wrong," I agree with Prince that we are conditioned to have at least two (and there can be more) opposing aspects of our personalities, making it difficult to accept our innate goodness—our belovedness. These opposing aspects explain why so many of us struggle with successfully doing the right thing even when we know the right thing to do. But I would argue that it is our propensity to err that motivates us toward "divinity." If we are aware of the wounds we have created on ourselves and others, the pain of carrying those wounds can become so burdensome due to guilt. We might also experience perceptions and misperceptions about our being, shame, and the isolation that comes from wounded people not wanting to be around us, all of which can make us give up on soothing our own pain. Instead, we seek succor from human beings and other visible life forms (often unsuccessfully). And sometimes, in an act of faith, supplication, or desperation, we lean into, with eyes and heart more widely open, the divine world. Our surrender to otherworldly realms, sometimes, is the only thing left to do when all conventional means of relief have failed.

TRIGGER WARNING: For a very brief moment, if it is not triggering, think about sex from the most pornographic perspective you can muster. Then, immediately bring to mind how you feel about virginal qualities. What's happening inside of you, *Dearly Beloved*? I do not want to deny the possibility of the connection between unconditional positive regard, vulnerability, eroticism, and spirituality. Prince, having grown up in a belief system that taught that human beings are born with a tendency toward being evil, still proclaimed that we are Dearly Beloved. In his bouncy song, "I Wanna Be Your Lover," Prince wrote that he wanted to be the kind of lover who also loved as a sibling and as a parent would. Prince was not writing and singing about incest but about treating his Dearly Beloved, who in this case was someone who he was also sexually attracted to, with every relational vantage point of love available to him—from agape to eros. He wanted his Dearly Beloved to be thoroughly loved and he was willing to embody whatever relational quality was needed. In this way, I see Prince as not all that dissimilar to other preachers of love, like even Jesus himself. Perhaps Jesus has that "preacher in the boudoir" kind of appeal for his followers. I apologize to all who need to believe that Jesus was without sexual appeal. I truly have no opinion on the matter. Prince, on the other hand, was hardly an angel of chastity.

What is important here is the message of universal love. Please use your imagination to take that in and visualize yourself as part of a global family. You are loved with the love of parents, their parents, their parents, your aunts and uncles, your siblings, and cousins who existed long before you were a twinkle in anyone's eyes. These people, real or imagined, need not be your immediate blood relatives but the embodiment of loving relatives irrespective of proximity or DNA. Caught in that visualization, there is no escaping the love that comes from intimate belonging and recognition, even when it feels too much to bear. We can shut down to the experience, but shutting down doesn't cut us off from the reality of our interconnectedness across generations nor our places in the legacies of future generations. To be Dearly Beloved is like being called by your true essence name—the one you were named before your essence was reduced to a conventional name. Your conventional name denotes your belonging to your physical and biological family, but your true essence name connotes your belonging to a broad and radically loving family of sentient beings, most of whom are not human.

Is this too far out? Not for Prince. He was concerned about humanity and other species. He was said to be vegetarian, vegan, or pescatarian; we can read in the book of Daniel how eating a vegetarian diet can lead to dream interpretations. He was also concerned, maybe even obsessed, near the end of his career, with our continued existence in realms beyond our ability to conceptualize the afterworld—what many call heaven.

Many Christians believe that Jesus willingly allowed himself to be murdered, knowing his spirit would return to heaven and then back to earth for his Second Coming. Many also believe he was born of a virgin, impregnated by Creator God. Think again about how a virginal quality and godly parentage emotionally lands on you. It is said in the Bible that God gave his only begotten son to humanity because God loved humanity so much, he would sacrifice his beloved son for our sake. In this understanding of God and Jesus, God is the ultimate lover of people, Jesus was his Dearly Beloved, people were Jesus's Dearly Beloved, people who encountered Jesus knew they were his Dearly Beloved, and eventually, through the history of Christianity, the concept of unconditional love, through sacrifice and resurrection gave breath to the concept of being reborn in Christ, saved from sin by Christ. This powerful archetype (and there are many) is what Prince, the preacher in the boudoir, stepped into when he sang "I Will Die 4 U," singing that he is the sacrificial messiah willing to die for his *"Darlin'."*

Stop. Wait for it. Did you feel it?

I apologize again for the interruption, but being in the emotional state of understanding one's own preciousness, vulnerability, fragility, tendency for error and simultaneously being understood as a Dearly Beloved darlin' can shift one's consciousness. Prince wanted his fans to believe and act out of their preciousness because he truly believed humanity would be destroyed in a horrific apocalypse, except for those who could live into their sacredness and be adjudicated as worthy. Prince believed Jesus would return to earth as he sang in "The Cross." Prince wants us to know Jesus's story of crucifixion and resurrection is our salvation if we can abide with suffering until his Second Coming. However, according to John of Patmos's dream in the book of Revelation, when Jesus arrives, it will be with much violence, physical destruction, and the killing of billions of people. It may seem paradoxical that our preacher in the boudoir believed so many of his beloved would be condemned, but I argue that this and every song referenced in this book should be taken in the context of deep compassion with the knowledge that Prince shared his message of belovedness because he desired for each and every one of us to live in paradise forever.

The prodigious quality of Prince's persona created an air of mysticism. He imbued every element of his art (persona, alter egos, fashion, lyrics, character development, screenplays, directing, choreography, acting, album cover concepts, playing multiple instruments, acting, etc.) with religious and spiritual symbolism. On the back cover of his self-titled album, he sat naked atop the Greek mythical winged white horse Pegasus, which represents an artistry, a power, and a method to get to heaven. He wore preacher's garb on his *Controversy* album, but underneath the same coat he wore a thong on his *Dirty Mind* album cover. On the cover of his *Lovesexy* album, he is totally stripped down, as he often asked his songs' characters to do or did himself, his bare behind situated in the ovule and ovary of the flower, looking upward as he often did as a posture of looking toward God, with the fingers of his right hand covering his left nipple. Typically, men don't cover their bare nipples. His legs and arms have no hair, but there is hair on his chest and abdomen. Does this image represent pure innocence? Is it the interpenetration of nature and man? The oneness of creation? Gender fluidity? Can we represent various facets of humanity and still feel like a Dearly Beloved?

These images, plus the one he stylized by combining the Westernized cultural symbols for female (a circle on top of a plus sign) and male (a circle with an arrow jutting outside), contributed to the overall self-image he cocreated with his fans: the international or universal lover, the embodiment of the Creator-Savior. This symbol represents the union and unity of binaries.

In addition to the white-winged horse and water archetype is the ankh symbol, which after being redesigned, became Prince's "name" during contractual conflict with Warner Brothers. The ankh is the Egyptian symbol for life, universe, and humanity. Prince used it in a more stylized form in the movie *Purple Rain* several years before he had it restyled, some say masculinized, to represent the harmony of female and male energies and principles. The ankh archetype represents the Egyptian goddess Isis, but I do not know whether Prince knew of this association. Prince was the consummate artist—one who recognized the artistic and archetypal power of ancient symbols and incorporated, restylized, repurposed, redefined, reinterpreted, and returned those symbols to his fans, oftentimes with himself in relationship to those symbols.

Sex, Salvation, Titillation

Through his use of "Dearly Beloved," "darlin,'" or "dear," Prince embodied a sensuous beguilement. I don't think it was always clear what he was inviting his audience into, but he had a way of capturing one's attention through a mix of endearment, enticement, titillation, seduction, and unconditional love. It is no wonder he was so controversial. Can we be endeared to someone we've never met, are unlikely to meet, in a very vulnerable way, with just one term of endearment? Apparently, we can, especially if that term comes from someone we are convinced is sincere in their sacrificial love. What creates that kind of sincerity? Prince, in the true form of a pied piper (perceived as good if you loved him and evil if you didn't) used terms of endearment over and over again, unconditionally it seemed, over a recording career spanning thirty-eight years beginning with his first album titled *For You*. Little did we know then that he was setting the stage for nearly forty years of explicit and many, illicit, love affairs with his fans.

Although Prince seemed to be steadily busy in his love of humanity project, through the use of terms of endearment and more, his song "Darling Nikki" illustrates the complexity and challenge of loving "that" which society deems as disordered and criminal. "Darling Nikki" is a song about a prostitute acting out of her most primitive sexual urges, crudely, in public—a hotel lobby—not the typical private boudoir where such acts, only between consenting lovers, belonged. However, "Darling Nikki" does invite her soon-to-be sex slave to her castle replete with devices to show him a funky good time. In this boudoir, the sex subject, Prince, was unable to make the castle a temple. He was unable to tame Nikki into a spiritual devotee. Nikki knocked him out and then vacated the premises. Is the absence of a redemptive quality in this song, or a lack of understanding that a redemptive project was in the making, the reason why Prince was scapegoated by politicians? He was met with so much disgust and resistance that some politicians sought to shut him down with the chilling effect of labeling his music as unsuitable for minors. Of course, this had an impact on the entire recording industry. Prince was publicly villainized by politicians because they did not want young people to become prematurely sexualized through his enticements.

This was 1984. Ronald Reagan was president of the United States from 1981 to 1989, and his election was, in part, a backlash to the Studio 54–like disco and cocaine years of the 1970s that preceded Prince. Prince tapped into the end of this largely lyrically vapid era in music and culture with a no drug use, racially inclusive, and pornographic punk messianic aesthetic and ecstatic dance message. Is it any wonder people like me, my college friend Debbie, and millions of others enthusiastically responded to being addressed as "Dearly Beloved?"

Prince's lyrics were Christian and hypersexualized. That drove social Christian conservatives crazy. Prince was "persecuted," crucified on the cross of sexual mores and freedom of speech and art, but through the power of the Purple Rain trilogy (song, album, and movie), Prince was resurrected by his fans from the tomb of the conservatism of the US political elected class. In short, when politicians sought to close the tomb by curtailing his free speech rights, his fans reopened it through their voracious consumption. To quote the Roxie Hart character in *Chicago*, the audience loved him, he loved them, and they loved each other because that's how showbiz is. The persecuting politicians wanted to prohibit children and youth from becoming his followers. This led to Tipper Gore, the wife of then vice president Al Gore, to participate in creating the Parents Music Resource Center in 1985. PMRC was responsible for creating Parental Advisory stickers, warning parents that music with the sticker was probably not appropriate for their children. It is possible that PMRC's efforts backfired, making Prince more popular than he already was. Why is that? Prince was not just a symbol of raw sexuality—he was also an evangelical Christian symbol. That is a very complicated mix of expressions in one artist.

Despite the efforts to demonize Prince, his appeal widened. Why would it not? He used a term of endearment, darlin', to sing about a woman who in real life would have been condemned to hell for sexually pleasing herself, arrested and imprisoned for indecently exposing herself, and committed to a mental hospital. Yet, she was a darlin'. Prince was someone who symbolized unconditional love and radical erotic lovemaking, breaking down the moral-immoral barriers between the two—like a Little Richard of his time, with alternating profane and angelic touches. He was bucking the social conservatism at the time and he was also bucking the Protestant Christianity of his youth. His Dearly Beloved darlin' project was a dissolution of polemics. Was it freeing? Dissolving opposites can be psychologically and emotionally freeing to such a degree that love can be felt and can emerge from the inside out. This is a practice I introduce in detail in chapter six.

As we know, Prince was no angel. Prince, the villain, continued using Christian tropes throughout his career steeped in sordid displays of sexual objectification. For example, he regularly evoked the rite of baptism in his art. In the Seventh-day Adventist tradition, people are baptized when they want to proclaim their old self is dead, they will no longer be enslaved by sin, and thus they are willing to be immersed in water to be clean and free. Seventh-day Adventists say, "I baptize you in the name of the Father, the Son, and the Holy Spirit. Amen." United Methodists also recite the baptism ritual in the trinitarian way and as a sign of God's grace. Prince in "Purple Rain" wrote that his ultimate desire was to see his beloved immersed in the Purple Rain. Then he asked for permission to guide his fans to the Purple Rain. Then, his fans chant, "Purple Rain, Purple Rain" with him. He invites his listeners into the temple of Prince, situated in the cesspool of life, to engage in a call and response, to signify (like a Black gospel kirtan of sorts) by asking his audience to raise their hands. In that gesture, like in yoga when we raise our arms above and open up our chest cavities to allow for deeper breathing, our heart space opens. The guitar solo is holy music. Even today, if you recognize talent on this scale, you will want to genuflect to his brilliance even if you abhor his erotic expressions or this theology. His vocalization is ecstatic, like he's filled with the Holy Ghost. Near the end of the song, you know you have arrived somewhere magical because of the twinkling and ephemeral sound of notes that sound like suddenly appearing and disappearing stars in the night sky. Prince was determined and persistent in his aspiration to take his Dearly Beloveds to celestial and sexual satisfaction.

Dorothy's Bathtub and Prince's Boudoir

Part of Prince's artistic brilliance was refusing to be predictable. If his use of baptism in "Purple Rain" was innocent, the waters he waded in in "The Ballad of Dorothy Parker" were not, at least not initially.

The beginning of the song is the beginning of a story about a woman who is also intelligent—a departure from how women were typically depicted in the younger Prince's songs, like, for example, the not-too-bright *Raspberry Beret* woman. Prince usually wrote about a woman's physical attractiveness. But not in "The Ballad of Dorothy Parker." This song is rare in that Prince describes the woman as a human being. She's not a car as in *Little Red Corvette*, she's not a hat as in *Raspberry Beret*, she's not a musical instrument as in a *Tamborine*, and she's not reduced to a sex organ only present for another's sexual gratification. Dorothy has a job as a night waitress. Her hair is of a certain color, she is tall, and she is successful in her work as a waitress (if getting many tips is a reference to the money she earns).

In the song, Dorothy approaches the customer for his order and then teases him about his choice of only fruit cocktail. She doesn't know that before she approaches him for his order, he has been engaging in an intensely conflictual internal dialogue *with* his past lovers. As a pastoral counselor, and a human being myself, I know that intensely conflictual internal dialogues are a sign that we have internalized into our consciousness strong emotions, unresolved conflicts, regrets about what was and wasn't said, loss, shame, confusion, and so on. All of which contribute to what Prince called "the violent room." We are all prone to violent room moments. So, the intelligent waitress, taking an order of fruit cocktail from a conflicted man, possibly reads the expression of the violent room all over his face and teases him by calling into question his manhood (as he contemplated his *ex*-lovers) while also letting him know that he's attractive. Seemingly her timing was just right because Prince wrote that the man needed someone wittier than himself to release him from his violent room. He got what he wanted, and what he didn't expect.

Dorothy, one of Prince's beloveds, invites her customer into her boudoir to take a bath. We can assume from the story that he had an erotic response to her teasing him about his fruit cocktail manhood on one side and his attractiveness on the other side. She entices him with a bind of opposites while he is already in his violent room. Conflicted, he accepts her invitation with a caveat: he agrees to get in the tub but with his pants on because, like a tempted and weakened preacher in the boudoir would, he would cross the sinful chasm while also being chaste. The song also makes clear that despite the violent room of ex-lovers, he also has a present lover. Dorothy is witty, so she calls him out on his strategy and again sarcastically says to him that he's acting like a real man. She doesn't stop there—she wants the pants off.

Dorothy, the intelligent, witty, and persistent seductress asks if she can turn on the radio. Lo and behold, her favorite song, Joni Mitchell's "Help Me" is playing right where Mitchell sings, "Help me, I think I'm fallin' in love." What great timing! Her phone rings and she ignores it, reminding her past customer and present prey that the caller can't be as attractive as who is in her bathtub. He surrenders and takes off his pants. Prince writes that Dorothy was unable to fulfill her sexual conquest in an idiomatic expression about Dorothy not seeing the movie because she had not yet read the book, meaning she was not wise enough to anticipate the future. She realized her ways and pretended that a witch's curse blinded her. In short, she knew she was doing wrong and her would-be prey was relieved with so much joy that he, who had been the subject of her fruit cocktail real man wit, laughed at her failure to victimize him. Through this joy, he was able to take another bath with his pants back on, clearing his violent room of noise and conflict, providing the peace of mind that gave rise to the wisdom to be quicker to resolve his dilemmas.

"The Ballad of Dorothy Parker" is not a *Kama Sutra* vision of enlightenment but is more like a Spooky Electric moment. Living a life of sin or redemption is where The Great Controversy concept takes root in one's consciousness, giving rise to conflicting desires and moral dilemmas. Yet, in genius Prince fashion, Dorothy's target in his most vulnerable state is able to turn the boudoir into the temple right after he takes his pants off! Prince, the pied piper could lead one to the Purple Rain, help resolve the conflicts in the "violent room," and also bring comfort to the afflicted, but his darlin' Dearly Beloveds might have to have a boudoir experience before they enter the temple. Maybe depending on what happens, one awakens to the fact that the boudoir has always been a temple—at least from a *Kama Sutra* perspective. From a Christian perspective, Prince's lyrics in "The Ballad of Dorothy Parker" indicate a willingness to be more aligned with Christian teachings on monogamy, but with a *Kama Sutra* sensibility, indicating that he is ready to consider taking more responsibility for his sexuality choices, with the help of God, by not being a slave to sinfulness and a helpless victim to seduction.

Love, Birth, Death

In his song "Sometimes It Snows in April," Prince sang that his darlin' dear beloved Tracy—a name he used for Jesus, as in "Christopher Tracy's Parade"—is someone who suffered, is truly missed, but may be happier in heaven because their questions about their suffering of loneliness on earth have been answered. The hope is that death does not keep us permanently apart. With this song, Prince is a compassionate comforter to his darlin' beloved.

Is Prince talking about a friend in the way we think about a flesh and blood human being with whom we are in a largely affirming relationship? Is he embodying Mary Magdalene comforting Jesus after he was crucified? The snow in April is a paradox—a chill in springtime, a reason to bring joy and sadness into dialectical tension, leaving one with a feeling of equanimity. Being a Dearly Beloved is also like feeling equanimous. April snow is representative of life where we experience both joy and sorrow, but without being known as another's darlin' Dearly Beloved there is mostly snow—it is Minnesota cold. The term of endearment brings joy amid isolation and alienation when what is deep in the heart of humanity are belonging and connection.

Prince used elements in nature, like rain, water, snow, and sunshine to signify God's essence. In his song "Play in the Sunshine," he invites, as an imp would, his darlin' Dearly Beloveds into the sacred end-times dance where they will bask ecstatically in the sunshine of glory, to dance as if it will be their last opportunity to enjoy each other fully, without the obscuration of intoxicants. The song "1999" offered the same invitation, to realize we are here now, but—always that "but," which was alluded to throughout his recording career.

In "Diamonds and Pearls," Prince wrote to his darlin' beloveds about his proclamation that he would never abandon them, that love would reveal everything they had been looking for and would even heal the colorblindness of their prejudices. When he wrote about diamonds and pearls in "International Lover," it was to seduce a woman to have sex with him. Prince, through the years, using the same words, could convey opposite meanings. Was he trying to redeem the lyrics of his earlier years? Not line by line but maybe album by album.

This is key.

Prince, a Black man, fought early in his career not to be typecast and reduced to a "Black musician" playing only R&B on Black radio stations. He resisted objectification. His band, The Revolution, was multiracial and they played rock, funk, R&B, pop, and their unique and special brand of gospel. He created a diverse fan base, and part of Prince's love for diversity was teaching his fans to release their conventional notions of identity, especially based on race, and embrace one another as each other's darlin' Dearly Beloveds. Before Prince died on April 21, 2016 (for his fans, perhaps the biggest April snowfall of all), of an accidental drug overdose (maybe a consequence of the scourge of fentanyl, the maintenance of celebrity status, or both) in the Temple of Paisley Park, a tragic and shocking irony occurred in light of what Paisley Park (the album, studio, and community) represented. After his death, it was rumored that he had countless songs stored in his vault. The invitations to be his darlin' Dearly Beloveds are also in many of his songs, for example in "7" he sings, "I'm yours now" and in "Diamonds and Pearls," "I will never run away" Prince seemed to be as devoted to his darlin' Dearly Beloveds as he was praying that his fans be devoted to God. He wanted his fans to be better able to create a temple within their own boudoirs—going straight to the heart.

***

The angel Aura in *Graffiti Bridge* was perhaps Prince's most darlin' Dearly Beloved. Aura died after she sacrificed herself to resolve the tensions between The Kid (played by Prince) and Morris (played by Morris Day) and their rival clubs, Glam Slam and Pandemonium. The Kid and Morris recognized their complicity in Aura's death, representing the death of love, due to their competitiveness and spiritual waywardness. Her sacrificial death (by intentionally walking into the street in front of an oncoming vehicle) is witnessed by The Kid, Morris, and members of the various clubs. The witnessing of her death leads to their reconciliation and everyone becomes darlin' Dearly Beloveds to each other.

We are all trying to get through this thing called life—a boudoir like Darling Nikki's castle and like Dorothy Parker's bathtub. Sometimes, a Little Red Corvette sidles up to us sideways (and they are still a Dearly Beloved person), but there's the possibility of turning the race car into a cab—transportation to a temple or the temple itself. Sometimes, we can't convert the boudoir into a temple because the funk of the situation overwhelms us so much that it makes our heads spin, but sometimes, we have the presence of mind to leave our pants on in the bathtub because we recognize we have commitments beyond the present tempting situation. It helps to remember that we have darlin' Dearly Beloved people to whom we are endeared and devoted. How might we understand ourselves to be loveable, just as we are? Does it help when we listen to "I Wanna Be Your Lover"?

Now, imagine Prince saying to you that he wants to be your lover.

Stop. Wait for it. Did you feel it?

How did it make you feel to imagine Prince, who called his fans "Dearly Beloved," also think of his fans as potential or imaginary sex objects? Some might find it creepily disorienting, teetering on the verge of betrayal, but others might find it perfectly congruent because platonic agape love can turn erotic, and with Prince, especially Prince the trickster, one might not know what kind of love Prince is proceeding with nor what kind of love it will become or return to.

Prince wrote and sang many lover songs as the priest and practitioner of *Kama Sutra*. As I mentioned in the introduction, I, and probably hundreds of thousands of others, was introduced to Prince, the unapologetic lover of sexual pleasure, on the Black radio stations in the United States. Prince's first hit was "Soft and Wet," where he sings about his lover having an orgasm, followed by "I Wanna Be Your Lover" which solidified Prince as an artist to contend with on Black stations, and introduced Prince as a pop artist on what were considered "white" stations. These songs set the stage, and expectation, that the Black Prince of the *Dirty Mind* was what we should come to expect. However, he released *Controversy*, *1999*, then *Purple Rain*, making him an artist of sex, R&B, and pop and of moral, spiritual, and political significance, complexity, and international acclaim. When he sang "Dearly Beloved" those of us churched people who heard it, I believed, received a blessing we didn't immediately understand—that we could be kinky and loved unconditionally—and that posed a threat to those in power who had preached the opposite for centuries. We could be beloved, the objects of eroticism, rejoice in it, and not fear

God's eternal punishment. What were we to do with this kind of revelation?

Ah, God Kama!

The purpose of the *Kama Sutra* according to Vatsyayana, and translated by Richard Burton, Bhagavanlal Indrajit, and Shivaram Parashuram Bhide, is mastery over the senses, especially sexual passion. When one becomes a master of their sexual impulses and behaviors, then, according to the sutra, they will be successful in everything else they do in life.

The *Kama Sutra* says there are nine types of intercourse corresponding to nine types of passion, but for purposes of this book, I want to focus on attracting one's sex partner, since Prince, the lover, was engaged in the art of attraction. In the *Kama Sutra* is a list of sixty-four arts or skills a man should be proficient in to be sexually successful with women. The first four include: singing, playing instruments, dancing, and doing all three simultaneously. Check, check, check, and check. In Prince's song "Gett Off" with Eric Leeds and others, he wrote about engaging in twenty-three sexual positions in one night! (I also find it very interesting that in this song he talks about consent, and that he will only get off with permission. Permission and consent are central to *Kama Sutra* practice.) Twenty-four positions or twenty-three, the point here is that Prince was influenced by the *Kama Sutra* and used pieces of it in his art and life as an artist and as a prophet of eroticism.

Here are some of the instructions. Men should be:

- well-versed in the science of love
- good storytellers
- able to inspire confidence in women
- articulate
- engaged in activities that the man enjoys
- devoted to sexual pleasures
- liberal

What I find most interesting about Prince's references to the *Kama Sutra* is the possible influence of the teachings on the art of seduction because Prince, in my view, was deeply and persistently engaging in the creation of a persona and artist who was a beguiling, polygender-expression, whore-like pious pimp who, in one song, could promote chastity and freakiness. "The Ballad of Dorothy Parker" is a perfect example, but from a *Kama Sutra* perspective, there is no separation between sexual pleasure and religious devotion—they are one and the same. This one and the sameness was one of Prince's decades-long mission.

The *Kama Sutra* supports enjoyment and pleasure in the arts and studying the arts, including singing, writing, dancing, and playing musical instruments. The list is long. One activity on the list reminds me of Prince's genius, item 45, which reads:

The art of speaking by changing the forms of words.
It is of various kinds. Some speak by changing the

beginning and end of words, others by adding unnecessary letters between every syllable of a word, and so on.

The drawing of an eye instead of the use of "I," the number 4 rather than "four," the use of U rather than "you," and "R" rather than "are" in many of his lyrics demonstrates his use of item 45, as does the album title *LOtUSFLOW3R*.

***

Item 49 reads:

> Mental exercises, such as completing stanzas or verses on receiving a part of them; or supplying one, two or three lines when the remaining lines are given indiscriminately from different verses, so as to make the whole an entire verse with regard to its meaning; or arranging the words of a verse written irregularly by separating the vowels from the consonants, or leaving them out altogether; or putting into verse or prose sentences represented by signs or symbols. There are many other such exercises.

Prince and the NPG Orchestra recorded an instrumental album titled *Kama Sutra*, and there are references to the *Kama Sutra* in "We Can Fuck" on the extended *Purple Rain* album and "We Can Funk" on the *Graffiti Bridge* album.

In "If I Was Your Girlfriend," Prince sings about the barriers erected between female and male lovers, asking his soon-to-be lover if he can have access to her mind and heart as she would allow one of her girlfriends to have. He knew we were socialized differently and that sometimes women resist deep intimacy with men in ways they do not with women because women tend not to fear that other women will sexually take advantage of them. Part of Prince's sex appeal, I believe, was his "softer" appearance—straightened and femininely coiffed hair, eyeliner and eye shadow, closely cropped facial hair, skin-tight clothing, and a soft voice often paired with an unapologetic expression of sexual urges that men of his day would be applauded for, but women would be shamed and judged for, like the "Little Red Corvette" woman who uses men as evidenced by the way she approached her next lover with a bunch of used condoms. Or the "Raspberry Beret" virgin woman who, when it was warm, wouldn't wear much more than her hat. Prince sang that if he had the chance to have sex with her again, he wouldn't change a stroke and how one strokes during sex is of vital importance in the *Kama Sutra*.

Were You the Prince of Light or the Prince of Darkness?

In so many songs, Prince lays out part of his vision of humanity's challenges. He writes that everyone has a vice. His happens to be sex outside of marriage: Prince believed that God, in his Christian denominational belief systems, condemned it. When we take Prince's music as a whole, we see him weighing his human and sexual desires against the teachings of his formative Seventh-day Adventist tradition. But being raised Seventh-day Adventist wasn't just about sexuality; it seems it was also about being named Prince and the impact that had on his identity formation.

Prince was raised in the Seventh-day Adventist Church before being baptized as a Jehovah's Witness much later in life. In between inheriting his parents' belief systems and exercising his agency to embrace another tradition, he had an encounter with the *Kama Sutra*, an ancient Vedic (Hindu) scripture. What led to the founding of Seventh-day Adventists in the United States was the evangelical spirit carried over by European settlers and eventually passed down to Prince through his parents.

William Miller is one of the church's founders and took a special interest in the Bible's book of Daniel and its prophecies about end times. Prince inherited end-times theologies that fueled his music for decades. It is important to understand the book of Daniel to understand Prince's art: King Nebuchadnezzar ruled Babylon and was so disturbed by his dreams he demanded his wise men accurately interpret his dreams (or nightmares) or they would be executed by being burned to death in a furnace. Daniel offered an interpretation that amplified the king's stature and entitlement to power, so King Nebuchadnezzar responded positively to the interpretation and to Daniel, the interpreter.

Consequently, Daniel rose in the king's ranks, becoming a ruler of Babylon, and became such a trusted confidant that he was able to dissuade the king from killing the wise men who were unable to interpret the king's dreams. Unfortunately, King Nebuchadnezzar enjoyed the devotion of his followers such that he demanded they create a gold statue of a god he worshipped. He misinterpreted Daniel's interpretation and those who refused to worship the golden god would be burned to death. Shadrach, Meshack, and Abed-Nego, the wise men, refused to worship the statue, so they were thrown into the furnace, but they were not consumed by fire. They survived without injury. Seeing this, King Nebuchadnezzar converted to the wise men's god, but his conversion did not transform his aggression, for again he threatened to kill anyone who did not worship his new god. Daniel was called on to interpret another of the king's dreams. Having done so successfully, Daniel was promised to be clothed in purple and elevated to be a third governor. To be clothed in purple is the purple *reign* that perhaps inspired Purple *Rain*. In chapter 12, it is written:

> At that time Michael [the guardian *prince* advocate for Israel and archangel against Satan] shall stand up,
> The great prince who stands watch over the sons of your people;
> And there shall be a time of trouble,
> Such as never was since
> There was a nation. . . .
> But you, Daniel, shut up the words, and seal the book until the time of the end; many shall run to and fro, and knowledge shall increase"

We can see the words "prince" and "purple" and "reign" may have filtered down into Prince's life and art through the intergenerational transmission of a Judaism-informed and inspired religion, Christianity, in the forms of apocalyptic-inspired Seventh-day Adventism and later, Jehovah's Witnesses.

As the book of Daniel comes to an end, like other terrifying visions of apocalyptic endings in the book of Revelation, it is depicted with so much horror, terror, and everlasting pain, it is no wonder a believer, like Prince, inspired perhaps by Daniel the dream interpreter and archangel Michael would be at watch over his fans who he tantalized with sin and salvation.

It has been written that Prince was given his first name by his father, John Lewis Nelson, because his father had a musical group called the Prince Rogers Trio; by naming his son Prince, he would also be passing down, generationally, his unfulfilled aspirations. Given Prince's religious inheritance, I cannot help but wonder if the name Prince inspired Prince to be more than the carrier of his father's unfulfilled musical aspirations. Royal princes in Germany during the Reformation were guaranteed the right to religious freedom and attempted to protect that right for their subjects. They were the preachers of the day who adhered to the Augsburg Confession, also known as The Confession, which was a response to the alleged abuses of the Catholic Church. Reform and rebellion led to the creation of the Lutheran Church, and German princes played a pivotal role. Was Prince the inheritor of this religious legacy?

In an email exchange with the New England church historian Professor David Frank Holland at Harvard Divinity School, Holland wrote:

> Seventh-day Adventists remained rather consistent from the death of Ellen White (1915) to the end of the twentieth century. It went through many changes before that and some after, but in honoring White's legacy there was not a great deal of alteration in the decades immediately after her death. So, I would say that the Seventh-day Adventism of Prince's parents was in keeping with the church that existed in the last couple of decades of White's life.

Prince, at least as expressed in his early art, used his religious inheritance without the "legacy burdens" (a concept I explain in more detail later, but is in essence an inheritance that is more like a curse than a blessing) of antisemitic, anti-Catholic, anti-paganist, anti-universalist, and anti-spiritualist expressions. Did he purposely refrain from creating art that would separate us from each other because that is what he believed real princes in the name of Christ did and should do? Being raised Seventh-day Adventist, combined with his father's aspirations may have embedded in him a princely purpose that he grew into and embraced, far more expansive than the consequences of sin. Yet, in the mix was also the *Kama Sutra*. It can be a daunting task to get through this thing. Prince's offer? To preach in the boudoir, the cesspool, the den of iniquity. In "Do U Lie," he wrote that he thinks of his lover when he can't sleep in his "boudoir."

Taken literally, the song is about pining for a lover, but Prince, the "I Would Die 4 U" prophet of sacrifice channels Jesus and the Christian doctrine that espouses that "God so loved the world that he gave his only begotten son," saw all of life as a boudoir, full of temptation, sexual ecstasy, and a crucible where raw sexual urges could become agape love with the right blessing and alchemic ingredients. Why was a magical blessing in the crucible necessary? The nature of being human, in this thing, is being flawed, being flawed contributes to this pop life thing, yet it is our work to get through this thing before the pop life gets us.

Crucibles

Part of getting through this thing requires an attempt at undoing the work done by others to present an age-old unauthentic image of humanity that we mimic. This work is done in life and Prince uses various images of crucibles to describe life's pressures. A crucible is a container that can hold objects subjected to extreme pressure of heat that transforms the burned objects into something else. Prince, the artist, conceived of many types of crucibles whereby Dearly Beloveds pit spirituality against sexuality, as if in a container of fire, to reveal the newly formed truth of the matter and situation. What are these crucibles?

"Darling Nikki's" crucible was a hotel lobby and then a "castle," which was a boudoir of a sadomasochistic sort. Dorothy Parker's crucible was a bathtub. Lady Cab Driver's crucible was a taxi cab. In "Little Red Corvette," Prince takes the concept of a crucible further, fooling the listening public into thinking the place and the person are separate—a brilliant move of nondual artistry.

"Little Red Corvette" is not a car but a woman in heat, her engine on fire, and is unabashedly interested only in sexual satisfaction. She proves through her collection of used condoms that she will not belong to her next conquest and she doesn't belong to anyone else, but he, who's ready to have his "Private Joy" shared with her, thinks that maybe she's too fast for herself and for him. He fantasizes that he can not only rev her engine but also downshift the gears of her libido and redirect her urges toward him before she blows a gasket. Getting through this thing often involves going through multiple sex partners, the pain of objectification, and the delusion and distortion of objectifying others. In "Strange Relationship," Prince sings about not being able to see his sex object happy, yet hates seeing her sad after having taken her self-respect by using her—what a contradiction.

Despite the varieties of crucibles for resolving animal sexuality on one side, and devotion and ethical behavior on the other, the main crucible is this thing called life, full of so many temptations that the boudoir is not limited to a walled-in private space replete with a bathtub, sex toys, orgy partners, and so on. Prince mostly wanted people to be able to come into the crucible for dancing, partying, and enjoying music and each other up until the point of exploitation. Exploitation was not getting through this thing but giving in to it. Exploitation, I venture to say, is an anti-Christ in the demonic spirit of "Annie Christian" where Prince asks his listeners to chant, "ABSCAM!"

"Annie Christian" is on Prince's 1981 album *Controversy*. ABSCAM was the name given to a late-1970s, early 1980s federal investigation of elected political figures by the Federal Bureau of Investigation (FBI). Several members of the House of Representatives and a US senator were convicted. To get through this thing, corrupt politicians need to put their heads on the block, in short, resign, confess, be held accountable, and allow for the presence of love to connect with God, not government.

Here's the thing about the thing—it's not a thing. Whatever "it" is, it's constantly dynamic, so getting through this thing is never a straight line from A to Z, from Alpha to Omega, never in one vehicle with the same body and mind while young or middle-age. Each human life cycle, spiral, or zigzag presents its challenges, but the opportunity to surrender to God will always be there. For Prince, this "thing" is worthy of figuring out because once it is, then Dearly Beloveds stand a greater chance of gaining a deeper understanding, making more loving choices, and perhaps greater trust in those, Prince included, who are helping people be skilled in resolving "violent room" conflicts to live life more abundantly.

The practice is to renounce objectifying others and resist being objectified by others. In doing so, we reduce the power of exploitation and the delusion of race, acknowledge our birthright, the purpose of gathering, and understand life as it is—in renouncing and resisting. When we love ourselves and one another, we have a greater chance of creating good boundaries and reducing the intensity of our desires to get from others what they may not want to give. To know that we shine like "Diamonds and Pearls" and know that there is "Joy in Repetition" when we repeat, as a mantra, that we are worthy of love. To get through this thing requires questioning ourselves and reality, including the teachings we were gifted when we were young.

Through the Theology of Prince project, I learned that many Prince superfans were not just fans of his art but were his spiritual followers. Prince was their prophet, leading them to the psycho-theological integration of good and bad, specifically God as good and sex as bad. By putting God and sex in dialectical tension for nearly forty years of artistry, Prince helped his fans—as a prophet might—to know God as one who did not punish people because of their sexuality. Sexuality was, in his view, God-given. Was Prince informed by the tantric sex practices of Hinduism or Buddhism? Those of us who grew up in different generations, and those of us who grew up in religious traditions that were anti-recreational sex or anti-sex for pleasure, can probably imagine the power of integrating the poles of God and sex. Prince, through art, helped free some of his followers from shame.

Practices

Affirmations

An affirmation practice is a positive self-talk spiritual and psychological practice to support the engagement with and emergence of the love aspect of one's innate self. An affirmation is a word or words said silently or out loud whenever one doubts that they are loveable or cannot love others. Based on what we know about being human, we know that even within those who have committed heinous acts, there was a love object at some time in their lives—maybe even when they were committing violence. The young Prince encouraged his fans to engage in free and mostly consensual sex. I say mostly consensual because seduction (that runs the risk of manipulation) is arguably not consensual. Nevertheless, as Prince entered full adulthood, he saw that love was necessary to make sex more meaningful and maybe even more pleasurable. When he realized the meaning of love, his "Dearly Beloved" salutation was made in "Let's Go Crazy, Let's Get Nuts" before there was evidence that he truly knew what love was. So, incorporating true love into "Dearly Be*loved*" as a simple affirming self-salutation can be said to one's self as:

"_____ (recite your full name), you are dear and beloved." When you do this, notice whether there is resistance arising as emotion, constricting bodily tension, pieces of a narrative that contradict the affirmation, a past contrary memory, or another form of denial. Let the resistance arise and fade away. Bring a slight smile to your face in acknowledgment that that is just how your mind works, then say the affirmation again. I suggest using this affirmation throughout your entire life because you will benefit from taking responsibility for reminding yourself of your true nature and because, unfortunately, very few people, if any, will or can take that responsibility on for others.

Lovingkindness Aspiration

You may think of yourself as unlovable or unworthy of love. If you do, do you think this is a permanent situation even though your very self is impermanent? Please contemplate. You are here today, but . . . (that "but . . ." will be discussed in more detail in chapter three). Your presence is temporary and so is everything else about you, including the aspects of yourself you believe to be unlovable or unworthy of love. This temporary situation is an opportunity to admit to yourself that if you are unlovable or unworthy of love, that too is a temporary matter. So, incline your mind and heart, as you would toward a newborn baby in need of nurturance to survive, toward self-love with these words:

> May I appreciate this moment.
> May I recognize this moment as fleeting.
> May I recognize myself as temporary.
> May I recognize this moment is full of
>   opportunities.
> May I recognize this moment is full of potential.

May I feel the freedom that is mine.
May I come to know myself as loveable.

Recite this aspiration at least daily, and gently, until you feel ready to accept it.

Righteous Sexuality

This practice is not for people committed to celibacy but for people who want to and who are acting on their sexual impulses. Prince, throughout his career, expressed raw sexual desire and pitted that desire against the desire to be prepared for end times and the possibility of living forever in paradise based on God's grace. Prince espoused hedonism as well as the centrality of love in sexual relationships. He was influenced by reformist Christian traditions and the *Kama Sutra*. His music was profane and profound, nasty and inspiring. If we take Prince's art and life as a whole, which is really impossible to do, we can safely say that he rejected objectification (eventually), exploitation, and oppression. When engaging in the art of attracting others to you, seduction, sex, and what comes afterward, ask yourself whether objectification, exploitation, and oppression are motivating your thoughts, desires, and actions. If objectification is present, slow down the behaviors involved in attracting others to you. Ask yourself if you're really being authentic about who you are. If you're engaged in seduction, again ask yourself if you're truly being authentic. One way to be authentic is to know your true motivations and be transparent about those motivations with your sex partner(s). Exploitation and oppression should be avoided at all costs.

Letter Writing

It can be very difficult to love one's self. The internal saboteur can attack, unexpectedly, when the impulse to love presents itself. Like Prince, you can give your internal saboteur a name. Prince called his "Spooky Electric." Choose your name and then write it a letter, letting it know how it has and is operating in your life, then tell it to stop. Here's an example.

> *Dear Undries—*
>
> *I remember when I first met you, or should I say when I realized you met me. I had been nominated for a scholarship in high school—the only person from my school nominated. There I was, around a table with bank executives dressed in business suits and students from other schools who were there to tell the executives why they should be selected for the scholarship. A four-year ride! Do you remember showing up? We each had about five minutes to say something about ourselves. I was so relieved that we didn't have to talk long and that I would be the last one to speak, giving me the advantage of knowing what others said, and time to prepare my remarks. When it was my turn to speak and all eyes were on me, that's when I knew you'd met me and I*

you. You felt the urge in me to feel something positive about myself, and when I felt it arise, you closed my throat down so much that I didn't think I could breathe. I began to sweat and my mouth got dry all of a sudden. After all I went through to get to the table, you snatched the tablecloth right from under me. When I opened my mouth, I said, "Well, what is it you'd like to know about me?" People around the table were shocked. One person said that it was up to me what I wanted to share, and I could see the look on everyone's faces. They pitied me. You convinced me that I had nothing good to say about myself. I knew right then and there that I had lost the scholarship because I couldn't say anything positive about myself. That's just one of the ways you showed up in my life, and I'm asking you not to do that anymore.
Signed,
Learning to Love Myself More Everyday

2
We Are Gathered

Listen Along

7
1999
America
Annie Christian
Baltimore
Christopher Tracy's Parade
Condition of the Heart
Darling Nikki
Diamonds and Pearls
D.M.S.R.

> Free
> I Would Die 4 U
> Paisley Park
> Pop Life
> Purple Rain
> Sexuality
> Temptation
> The Cross
> The Ladder
> When Doves Cry

Dearly Beloved,

It is my hope that after reading the previous chapter, you will know that you are invited to pause, ponder, and accept that you are dear and beloved, which means you are vulnerable, precious, and worthy of self-love and self-protection—no matter what others think of you. Please take a moment to pause on this in case you forgot to do so.

In the Dearly Beloved chapter, I referred to a practice for you to get in touch with aspects of yourself that may have obscured your pristine nature. You were asked to write a letter to the personality or personalities that make an appearance to undermine your Dearly Beloved sense of self. If you wrote the letter, congratulate yourself for doing something that is often very difficult to do—facing the facts of our self-hatred and putting those facts in "undeniable" forms for the senses to take in and potentially metabolize into the power needed to connect the Dearly Beloved self with others, be they aware or actualized, or not.

Prince in his song "Let's Go Crazy" begins with the affectionate salutation and an invitation to prevent the causes of isolation—to gather together. You may think that with over eight billion people on earth, with many dying and being born every second, our presence on earth means we are gathered on this planet. But we are not gathered. Gathering is a dynamic bodily phenomenon that often includes charismatic leaders (but not always because a cause or mission can attract people to gather in support of that cause or mission) with an attractive mission (not always because some charismatic leaders are narcissists without a cause or mission beyond themselves), with the promise of something beneficial for those who come forward. Prince was a gatherer who sang about the value of gathering.

Gathering in Paisley Park

In "Paisley Park," Prince wrote about how loving people attract people who want to be loving. I invite you to imagine you are approaching a park you want to be in because you are curious about its reputation for attracting things. What things? People who are deemed strange by conventional standards; people with their hair swept back on one side. The year is 1985, and there are many different styles and expressions to appreciate. With this vision in your mind, notice your emotions, your bodily sensations, and other thoughts running through your head. Would you feel comfortable in a park of people unlike yourself or can you only have fun with people you deem like yourself?

Prince, the purple and paisley one, seemed to enjoy, embrace, and promote colorful people. He was not just promoting racial inclusivity but a diversity of styles and the unconventionally inclusive personalities that defied the social norms of the 1980s in the United States. Prince was masterful at offering lyrics that invited listeners to visualize. In his song "When Doves Cry," he invites an appreciative imagination. It's the willingness and ability to appreciate the vision and imagery offered that allows us to dig the picture, but it is trust and faith in the gatherer, the visionary, that sets the mind to see beyond the present moment and situation.

Returning to "Paisley Park," Prince wants us to imagine that the colorful and stylish are also deeply peaceful as evidenced by the smiles on their faces. This visualization could be jarring because this is not usually what happens in society because people of such differences are often individually at odds with each other or at odds with opposing groups. Too often, differences are interpreted as offensive and a threat to the "standard order of life" according to those with power, Prince referred to them as the ruling class, dictating how others should live and be. But the peace Prince describes in this park, with others different from themselves, is so profound they have no desire to be anywhere else, ever. Can you imagine such a feeling of contentment and commitment? This is the kind of gathering Prince preached no matter the den-of-iniquity boudoir he found himself in. But in this case,

Paisley Park was never the boudoir—it was imagined as an everlasting nirvana, a condition of the heart, in the heart.

Why a condition of the heart? In Prince's "Condition of the Heart," he sings about being a fool for unrequited romantic love, but the condition of the heart needed for being in the nirvana of "Paisley Park" is not romantic nor conditioned, if you will, on reciprocity. The girl on the seesaw is joyous because she is immersed in love, in a place where forgiveness is possible, where there's no financial exploitation from corporations or the government, no oppression, and where the admission is easy—in D.M.S.R. [Dance, Music, Sex, Romance], everyone, of different races and ethnicities, is invited to party and sing together in harmony.

Unfortunately, it is difficult for Europeans, Negroes (Prince's word), Puerto Ricans, Japanese, and people from all countries and continents to sing together or be in harmony with one another. Prince, who lived most of his life in the United States, and the Minneapolis area in particular, knew his country had systems in place that undermine the ability to be "we-are-gathered" people. In "America," he wrote that he wanted God's grace to keep us free people.

Free for what purpose? It is in divine order to have liberty of conscience and that means freedom from government-imposed religion. Also, freedom allows us to gather. The need to gather for the expression of freedom is so innate in our species, it is enshrined and codified in the First Amendment to the US Constitution as the right to assemble. The right to assemble is so taken for granted, maybe our assemblages are taken as natural law, transcending the

Constitution. But natural or unnatural law, the power of assemblage, being "we-are-gathered" people means we can do great charitable acts that have far-ranging consequences. Of course, the converse is true as well: we can engage in behaviors that cause catastrophic damage.

There's also the risk of objectifying others in the assemblage of gathered people. Prince wrote in "Temptation" that everyone has a vice; his happens to be the sexual urge that gets overly activated at an orgy. This is a song about orgies, a cesspool situation, and his obsessive compulsion toward kinky sex until the voice of God interrupts with the threat of death. Prince, who wants to live, repents and is freed of his lust. We don't know if the orgy ends, but perhaps the lesson here is that when the assemblage is a cesspool situation where others are objectified, the whole group, being reminded of the consequences of our actions, may break us out of groupthink, pack-like ravenousness. In between consuming others and waking up to our existential concerns, the fear of loneliness may present itself as a motivating factor in our behavior. Greed for others to satisfy our isolation may ironically and sadly recreate the alienation we fear. Prince was aware of this: in "The Ladder" he wrote about the possibility of feeling worthy and a part of God's creation that would decrease feelings of loneliness.

We are gathered in this holy assemblage not confined by the circumference of the planet, or even of space, but by the vastness of reality beyond our ability to comprehend. Yet, it is this lack of ability to comprehend that may prevent self-worth as a felt experience. It seems paradoxical, but maybe that is exactly what it takes to feel the cosmic interconnection that is our individual and collective experience.

Threats to Gathering

Why is it so difficult to be gathered? What are the threats to gathering? In "America," Prince, Robert Rivkin, Lisa Coleman, Matthew Fink, and Wendy Melvoin wrote that rich people distanced from everyday working-class people are so busy making wealth, their activities obscure the opportunity to be aware their time is just about up. Financial exploitation is a form of communistic repression that quashes individual artistic expressions and oppresses individualism in the interest of collective interests and expressions. A rejection of this financial exploitation is what led to the creation of the symbol that represented The Artist Formerly Known as Prince. This sort of exploitation was, for Prince, a sin much greater than orgies.

Threats to gathering prevent the creation of the Rainbow Children and one significant threat comes from those engaged in building a new nation based on a patriarchal structure: beginning with God, followed by a man, followed by his wife, then followed by their children. But Rainbow Children, Prince wrote, will keep God's covenant. I believe that in his song "7," Prince is suggesting that the covenant will be kept by resisting all the ways hatred is made manifest. To be gathered is not just to party like it's 1999, or the end of the world, or to rejoice by beholding Jesus in "Christopher Tracy's Parade," or to be tempted by orgies. Ultimately, to be gathered is to create a new enlightened society.

The Dearly Beloved who are gathered are to transform hateful culture through interracial communities devoted to love. In "Diamonds and Pearls," Prince, channeling his understanding of God's anti-racist and eternal love that will come with the Second Coming of Jesus, sings about a mind-blowing love that will make everything shine until we no longer see people as racialized human beings.

I don't think it can be overstated that whatever Prince was writing and performing, anti-Black racism was core to his art. Even in the song "Sexuality," he sings that we must become organized to address racialized segregation. Gathering with this intention and commitment is how to make the most of the gathering, but the energy of the gathering is not to be limited to those present. The energy is to be converted to power, expressed internally and externally, as represented in Prince's song and group "New Power Generation." The purpose of new power, or regenerativity, is to push through old forms of being and expression, including the generational abuse of power, to love more imaginatively and vibrantly.

For example, in "Family Name," he lays out a systematized way of understanding one's Black-bodied self from the pejorative label "minority" to a godly people "the Tribe of . . .". For Prince (be he prophetic, messianic, or mentor), altering consciousness around racial classifications, hierarchies, castes and the like is central to the salvific message that he could at least assist in leading his fans out of the pop life and into Paisley Park.

This is also what gathering in his song "D.M.S.R." is about. Inspired by "D.M.S.R.," I propose a mantra and chant: "Everybody, everybody, people everywhere." Say it once when you feel separated or alienated from others. Say it a few times, as in a chant, to readjust your consciousness toward being aware of your interconnected nature. Mantra or chant, let it guide you toward the inclusive vision of Purple Rain. What is the Purple Rain as it relates to gathering? It's Paisley Park, the place where colorful (including "purple" and the paisley combination of colors) people can see others laughing and bathing in a transcendental experience something beyond conventional descriptions. The Purple Rain is the Paisley Park is the Rainbow People. People willing and able to harmoniously be together with their differences, inspired by appreciation for difference, with a commitment to love, enjoy one another, and be concerned about the welfare of all. As we will soon discuss, even when these factors are present, there still remains the challenge of moving from insecure introversion (a fear-based detachment from others) to secure extroversion (a risk-taking or courageous attempt to relate to others) to contribute to and receive the fruits of being gathered.

Prince was also a social critic concerned about the abuse of power—governmental and corporate—to keep people apart from each other and doubtful of their own innate worth and lovability. The abuse of power creates the chilling effects (self-imposed limits on free and responsible speech and creative expression) that can lead to artistic incarceration—creating art within the confines of what powerful taste arbiters demand—and causes the conditions for creative exploitation and spiritual enslavement as evidenced by the word "slave" written on Prince's face during the period of his contractual battles. Many of us duck and hide inside our heads, in insecure introversion, to feel a secure invisibility. We intentionally reduce contact with others and consequently undermine our ability to be intentionally gathered. Authoritarianism that is not publicly resisted can exacerbate insecurity and introversion, but there is an alternative—extraordinary extroversion.

Extraordinary Extroversion

As I see it, people who are living into extraordinary extroversion can be introverts or extroverts (just as extroverts can choose to live in insecure introversion), but extraordinary extroverts choose to go beyond their psychological comfort zones to intentionally build community, be in solidarity, publicly speak the truth, take risks in saying what is wrong—TO BE A WITNESS—and lean into protecting others. This is the potential power of being gathered and may explain the intense love and devotion Prince's fans had and still have for him.

Prince performed live as a *lifestyle* and profession. One glance at his concert schedule between 1979 and 2016 on Princevault.org and one will be amazed at how extraordinarily extroverted Prince had to be to push through his introversion to perform live at that rate. When he was at home at Paisley Park, he hosted parties and concerts and invited people who were from the community—not just members of his entourage. But not all concerts were for the same purposes. He performed in a concert in Baltimore after unarmed Black man Freddie Gray was killed by police. He also performed at the White House when Barack Obama was president. Live concerts were his mode of extraordinary extroversion; one need not be an extrovert to engage in the risk-taking kind of courage to push through the fears and insecurities that lead us to disconnect from one another.

How do we practice extraordinary extroversion in a chilling speech context that would otherwise undermine our desire to be gathered? Take a quiet moment and feel into any sense of loneliness, isolation, and alienation that you chronically experience. When you feel the suffering of it and you feel like you understand it, begin to shift your imagination to experience the joy you might feel in being at ease with others around you. Ask yourself, "What are we enjoying together?" If what is being enjoyed results in hurting others, imagine what other steps you might take to go from insecure introversion to extraordinary extroversion. Is it sending a text, an email, or making a call to someone whose company you enjoy to say, "Hey, I'd like to have fun with you. Are you open to that?" Or doing a bit of research on something you enjoy, like live music, and going to a concert with many fans unknown to you, with the thought that you can enjoy something with others gathered, without the condition of knowing anyone? As you build your experiences and confidence in being gathered, experiencing shared joy, you are potentially moving toward the extraordinary extroversion that amplifies the experience, meaning, and purpose of gathering—to get through this thing called life as an individual and as part of a collective.

Re-Awakening the New Rainbow Sibling Revolutionary Generation

Human beings are an interesting species because we have the capacity, we believe, to achieve higher states of intelligence, awareness, and consciousness. On the one hand, we are unable to collectively and globally create and sustain these achievements without communication, respect, recognition, negotiation, wealth distribution, and accountability. On the other hand, I have seen how a response to an event can reveal that we are able to engage in short-term collective and collaborative awakenings with complete strangers.

After unarmed Black man George Floyd was tortured and murdered in Minneapolis, Minnesota, on May 25, 2020, Prince's Paisley Park Rainbow Children throughout the world immediately responded *together*. No one knew this atrocity was going to happen, but while it was happening in broad daylight while being recorded on cellphones by people trying to prevent torture and murder, people throughout the world reawakened to the rising increase in blatant police violence against Black people throughout the world and the history of colonization and decolonization.

Police reforms took place, and per usual in the United States, a backlash against police reforms also took place. In the United States, the backlash has included an attack against public school boards, public school teachers, public libraries, and public librarians. It is anti-publican in that people are turning against the very people, our neighbors, needed to foster and maintain democratically run republican states. This distrust of each other undermines our ability to gather. These attacks have been labeled as "anti-woke," meaning legally prohibiting speech that informs government-funded institutions and their constituents, including public school students, that slavery in the United States was brutal. It would do us well to pay close attention to any policy that is anti-awareness of what is factual.

The governmental threats to all people becoming aware of history and brutality means it is not enough to be Paisley Park attendees on the seesaw nor the Rainbow Children delivering the covenant. We will always need to be re-awakening because there will always be efforts to make us fall asleep. Think of Prince's groups and collaborations—The Revolution, New Power Generation, 3rdeyegirl. And there were groups he didn't perform with. Being here and awake today comes with changes, challenges, obstacles, and opportunities.

Being gathered may mean letting go of communities and joining new ones. Spiritual practices, especially contemplative ones, support flexibility and adaptability. My hope is that by imagining ourselves as a New Rainbow Sibling Revolutionary Generation *at this time*, we will keep pushing the needle in the Funkadelic "One Nation Under a Groove" song that proclaims humanity's capacity to be new breed leaders (borrowing from Prince's song "Sexuality") standing up to organize, persevere, and become enlightened. Proclamations, no matter how funkily rhythmic they are, are not enough though. We need to be in relationship with others, advocating for a refreshment in the old ways we deny each other's humanity. To that end, based on the Theology of Prince project I headed at United Theological Seminary of the Twin Cities, I was invited by Build Up to give a talk on the Theology of Prince and on how his art might inspire their activists. Build Up is an organization of international activists who use technology to create conditions for the peaceful resolution of harmful conflicts. When I received the invitation, my initial internal response was insecure introversion. It is my nature to avoid public speaking because initially I usually don't think I have anything to say that hasn't been said or can't be said better by others (that's how my internal saboteur shows up). I am a pastoral counselor who is comfortable listening to people in a dyad, triad, or small group. The invitation reminded me that I'm also an advocate and human rights activist who invested a lot of time, and money, into overcoming my insecure introversion. So, I was presented with this opportunity for extraordinary extroversion, to share Prince's art in a way I had not done so before, with an audience I had never met. There were about two hundred people present, and in essence, I shared that Prince called for new breed leaders that I thought Build Up exemplified. I talked about

Prince's experience of being financially exploited and the many ways he resisted corporate greed, even ownership, of what he thought should be his intellectual property. He supported the development and use of technologies owned by artists. I'm not a preacher, but I was there to inspire, so channeling Prince as much as I could, I asked the audience to repeat after me as I chanted from "Sexuality," "We need a new breed leader, stand up, organize."

I talked about Prince encouraging his fans to pay attention to the signs of climate destruction, threats of nuclear annihilation, and devolving mores around us to inform our activism, even though he believed it wouldn't save us from apocalyptic destruction. Build Up activists were well aware of the damage we do to each other as they worked against widespread oppression and violence, using new technologies to mitigate harm. I talked about how technology was fueling physical harm in Amazon's fulfillment centers and how employees had organized, become new breed leaders, for change. I asked them to reflect on their lives as if their life's album was about to be produced. Like Prince did with his crew when they had deep conversations about what they'd leave for the next generations, I asked Build Up activists to reflect on what they are leaving. I closed our time together with a prayer I wrote, in the liminal years between being a financial adviser and a pastoral counselor. I call it "Sermon on Mt. Wall Street":

> Worthy are the disinherited
> For their worthiness is not based on wealth

Worthy are those who grieve
For their grief can be turned to wisdom and action
Worthy are the betrayed
For their betrayal is evidence of their faith in
    goodness
Worthy are those who hunger for recompense
For they thirst for justice
Worthy are those who forgive
For they are free
Worthy are the whistleblowers
For they are soldiers for the truth
Worthy are the honest regulators
For they protect humanity
Worthy are those whose calls for transparency
    were ignored
        For Greed's sake
For the day will come when your calls are
    undeniable
Worthy are you when they minimize you, ostracize
    you, lie about
        You, and abandon you in your pursuit of
            justice
Take delight, Worthy Ones, for your rewards are
    beyond measure.
    (written in 2011, dedicated to Ponzi scheme victims
    and the Occupy Wall Street Movement)

After I gave my speech, the audience applauded and we had a robust Q&A. I was relieved to have worked through my insecure introversion to extraordinary extroversion, but I needed to rest. Pushing through our emotional and energetic nature requires energy that needs refueling, so please remember to rest and plan for rest every time you engage in extraordinary acts that push you beyond your habituated limits.

To be the "We-are-gathered" people takes more than just being present on earth. We are inclined to be in relationship with others for a purpose, mission, or cause, and in many unfortunate situations, to be the narcissistic supply for egomaniacs. Life, and getting through it, requires healthy gatherings to support one another, advocate for one another and the groups we belong to, and be visible to one another. Cultures are created by and maintained on gathering, and gathering can be used for constructive and destructive purposes. It has been a societal concern for some time that loneliness is becoming an epidemic. It is becoming known that loneliness is not just physical isolation but the cause of other ailments. Loneliness is not limited to old people who have survived the death of loved ones but is the result of parental and sibling neglect, bullying, loss, and being canceled. When the wounds that create loneliness fester, insecure introversion may be the result. Through faith in ourselves, others, and implementing spiritual practices to be engaged with others, there is a greater potential to move through insecure introversion into extraordinary extroversion and thus contribute to the gatherings that are constructive and support flourishing.

Practices

Visualization

After you read this practice, I invite you to record yourself reading it so you can play it back with your eyes closed:

Dig if you will an image. Waves of purple flowers. There is a smell like salty powder, so you take a deep breath in, noticing how your lungs expand and then contract to calm your entire body. The smell is tickling your tastebuds like a gumdrop. A bit of saliva collects in your mouth. You swallow it as if it is purple grape juice. The sky is clear, with clouds like big white rabbits and happy doves landing to surround you. You're lying comfortably in a chaise lounge, yellow sunbeams shining on your body, keeping you warm. No one is on the beach but you. The sound of ocean waves lulls you to deep relaxation while the balmy breeze of lightly salted air vanishes all anxiety. The smile on your face is slight, indicating profound inner peace. When you open your eyes, you see that people have entered the beach, laying on their own chaise lounges, taking in the same ocean, sky, sun, and breeze. No one looks exactly like you, but you all are sharing the same cosmic resources without depleting anything. Their inner peace, their joy, strengthens your inner peace and joy—your inner peace and joy strengthens theirs. Allow yourself to feel this throughout your entire body. Now, slowly arise from your chaise lounge and give a real cool "what's up I see you" nod to your neighbors on the beach. Feeling this connection to the universe, you make a vow to carry this vision throughout the day.

Extraordinary Extroversion

This is a relational practice, so get ready to imagine trusting others to help pull you out of the shell you've been in for fear of rejection. Feel how your insecure introversion impedes your ability to feel free and confident. Pay attention and accept the fact you've passed up many opportunities to more fully enjoy life because you were afraid of someone's judgment, rejection, or worse. Now, think about what you've learned from these experiences. If you had the opportunity to do things differently, what would you do, and why would you do it? Think about the many people in your life who have not hurt you, especially the ones who intrigued you, but you chose not to get to know them because you were afraid that once they knew the real you, they would reject you. Now, ask yourself if you want to live the rest of your life this way. Do you really want to live the rest of your life under a shell? If the answer is no, then make a bold move. Contact someone you've wanted to get to know and get to know them if they'll let you. Allow yourself to admit the truth that loneliness hurts and good friendships bring joy. Pay attention to what triggers your vulnerability. Decide if you want to be transparent about it without expecting your acquaintance to take care of it. Sense into how the two of you want to communicate in the future, how frequently, and for what purpose. Allow yourself to feel awkward. The point is not to convince yourself that you're invulnerable to embarrassment but to feel connected. As you feel into this, continue your outreach. To live joyfully with friends doesn't require having many friends.

As you gain confidence in practicing extraordinary extroversion, you may find that your confidence in being in platonic friendships may build your stamina to be in small groups of people gathered around a purpose and that your experience in smaller groups may lead to a greater ability to be in larger groups. The point in all of this is to come out of the shell more than you have in the past, keeping the shell for when you really need it, like if you're under attack in ways that could truly wound you.

Sympathetic Joyful Aspiration

One of the ways living in insecure introversion clouds our perceptions and beliefs is by misinforming a comparing mind. We compare one thing against another to determine its worth, and unfortunately, we do the same to ourselves. This comparing mind can lead to envy, jealousy, judgments, prejudices, hatred, and alienating behaviors (to name a few). The comparing mind can contribute to the very thing we're trying to work our way out of—fear.

As you practice moving from insecure introversion to extraordinary extroversion, begin to imagine that everyone you know, everyone you're getting to know, and even yourself should have the opportunity to experience joy. As we develop the lovingkindness aspiration, we also develop the wholesome desire for people to feel joy, and as we develop the wholesome desire for people to feel joy, we cultivate the lovingkindness aspiration. Please allow yourself to imagine these feelings for others. Now, imagine yourself feeling joy just because someone feels joy. When you feel it, you've felt sympathetic joy. Here are a few phrases that may support this practice:

> May I allow my imagination, in this moment, to include people I know.
> May I allow my imagination, in this moment, to include people I do not know.
> May I allow my imagination, in this moment, to include myself.
> [Bring a slight smile to your face.]
> So many things in life bring people joy: [List a few.]
> May I celebrate the joy they feel when they experience joy.

3
Here Today

(But . . . You Have to Wake Up and Cross That Graffiti Bridge)

Listen Along

1999
Annie Christian
Can't Stop This Feeling I Got
Dreamer
Elephants & Flowers
Graffiti Bridge
Joy in Repetition
Love Machine
Melody Cool
New Power Generation

> New Power Generation, Pt. 2
> Paisley Park
> Purple Rain
> Release It
> Revelation
> Ronnie, Talk to Russia
> Round and Round
> Sexuality
> Shake!
> The Latest Fashion
> The Love We Make
> The Question of U
> Thieves in the Temple
> Tick, Tick, Bang
> We Can Funk
> When Doves Cry

Dearly Beloved, (pause)
    We (pause) are gathered (pause) here today (pause), but . . . (pause).

I put five pauses in a short sentence to help you slow down the process, observance, and meaning-making that goes into reading something that has the potential to be insight-producing and therefore life-changing. If you didn't experience insight, meaning-making, or the potential to change, I invite you to slowly read it again.

Dearly Beloved, (pause)
We (pause) are gathered (pause) here today (pause), but . . . (pause).

You are here today. You exist right now. These pauses, for reflection, are part of the practice of mindfulness. Mindfulness means paying attention to what is happening, as it is happening, as it stops happening, and with as little to no judgment as possible. It means to be aware of when you are creating a story that is not verifiable based on the facts or when an interpretation of the facts has become the only truth that can exist. The pauses are also for noticing the sensations that arise when you become defensive, releasing tension when defensiveness disappears, and ceasing the pursuit of delusive thought. Today, you are here, or there—somewhere at this fleeting time. You have a past. In your previous here moment, you were creating the immediate future moment that has already passed.

It is nearly impossible, maybe even impossible, to take in every moment. But Prince's music is an invitation to try to be awake to the fact that you, we, are here today, and that fact could end by the time you get to the end of this sentence, paragraph, or book. The symbol of the eye Prince frequently used is about paying attention to everything without prejudice. So, what can we use from his art to pay attention and improve our ability to do so—in the present moment? To see with as little prejudice as possible, let's begin with the origins of our belief systems that inform and impact what we believe.

Origins of Belief

As I stated at the outset, I was raised in the United Methodist Church; Prince was also exposed to United Methodist teachings. I was also raised in the church in the United States, where we have a culture of convincing children to believe in things that don't exist. The Easter Bunny, Santa Claus and the elves, the Tooth Fairy, and within subcultures, many other fantastical characters.

Why do we do this to our children, and they in turn do it to their children? We live in a culture of make-believe. The Walt Disney Company built a fantasy empire for children. Despite how prevalent science and scientific methods are for producing knowledge, there is an aspect of being human that wants a reality that isn't materially manifest. It is very difficult to be aware of being here today. Religion in the United States operates similarly—we often use fear to make our children believe so they will behave. Does Prince use fear to make us believe? Yes. The word "but" is a placeholder for the fear.

As a pastoral counselor, and someone years ago who knew people who took their lives, I know that not everyone will feel appreciation and comfort because they are here today. Some are elated about being here today, and others are counting the minutes, days, and years until the end. Yet, in Prince's belief system, to be here today is to be alive. To be alive is a temporary blessing imbued with free will and sexual urges, but . . . it is fleeting. That's a lot to figure out when you're young and don't know the first thing about death. That is why fantasy characters and religion can play such a defining role in a young person's life.

I'd like to return to the Easter Bunny, Santa Claus, the elves, flying reindeer, and the Tooth Fairy for a moment. In my childhood, I was taught that there was an Easter Bunny. The Bunny has nothing to do with Jesus's resurrection and apocalyptic Second Coming, so I learned nothing about Easter by believing in the Easter Bunny, who delivered colored eggs (we were never taught about the chickens who laid them) in a wicker woven basket full of fake cellophane grass and candy. Santa Claus, the elves, and flying reindeer, I was taught, were all part of the toy delivery system that entered our home without a chimney or a door key under the doormat to drop off the gifts we earned for being good children. If we weren't good children, we would be punished with coal or maybe worse—not get what we wanted or thought we deserved. One of the ways we were taught to show hospitality toward Santa Claus was to leave him cookies and milk on Christmas Eve. In the morning when we excitedly woke to open our gifts, we would check to see if Santa drank some milk and ate some cookies.

In retrospect, I can see how believing in Santa Claus helped me believe in God, but believing in the Easter Bunny didn't help me believe in Jesus's resurrection. The only thing that helped me believe in the Tooth Fairy was the desire for money, the loss of teeth, adults asking me if the Tooth Fairy had visited me, and the coins under my pillow that "magically" appeared. Boiled colored eggs in the spring, presents in the winter, and money every time a tooth falls out makes for a magical mindset and instills a bit of dread in parents who share these fantasies because they know one day their child will learn it was all a game.

Religion can be used in the same ways, but Prince's religion focused on the existential threat of God's annihilation, the gap between being here now for those who want to be, the "but" and fear between the two, and the desire to get our eggs, gifts, and money, see reindeer fly, and live life *forever*. In the West, we are primed by these conventional cultural slights of hand into believing that we can't live happily unless we get what we want. We learn to bargain, at an early age, with that which is greater than ourselves. That bargaining to get what we want out of life, avoid additional suffering, be reminded of our goodness, etc., remains a part of our being when we realize that getting what we want is beyond our ability to get it. Living happily with multiple disappointments is the "but" I want to explore in more detail. But first, Prince and his existential message.

The Graffiti Bridge Album

I think it is fair to say that "1999" (released in 1982) is Prince's most popular existentialist song. In it, he wrote about the real nature of life, its temporality, and war. The *Controversy* album (1981) is his tribute to The Great Controversy as he understood Seventh-day Adventism at that time in his life. Prince never abandoned the quest to resolve the questions that arose from contemplating the relationship between God and human beings, and who would be deserving destruction. At that time in his recording career, perhaps he had not offered a cogent collection of works to point his fans toward everlasting paradise. Maybe he wanted to put all of his thought into one project. Nearly ten years after *Controversy*, he released another trilogy, *Graffiti Bridge* the movie, album, and song.

The central message from each song on the *Graffiti Bridge* soundtrack amounts to this overall message: we need an angel to save us from the existential threat God has promised, so let's not be too comfortable that we are here today. The ". . . but" is like an injunction on our temporary joy, while also paradoxically is an invitation to everlasting joy. Which should we choose? Prince's mission was to help us choose everlasting joy, and on this, he seemed to never waver once he understood the meaning of true love.

On the *Graffiti Bridge* album, an album that has a narrative and theological arc, Prince begins with "Can't Stop This Feeling I Got," a song not only about being knocked down, out of control, and alienated but also about cultivating resilience and joy. The song title speaks to the power of being inspired, as I surmise, by the Holy Spirit. In short, the album begins with a song of hope. Why start with hope? Without hope, why would one listen to the rest of the album? There must be a reason to pursue everlasting joy, which is its own kind of delayed gratification, over the temporary ways we immediately but also temporarily satisfy our desires.

The album continues with several songs that keep us asleep and off the bridge. From hope and inspiration, Prince moves listeners into "New Power Generation," a song about sex, music, love, and resistance to conventional thinking and conventionally thinking people. Being here today means there will be conflict between people with power who want to hold on to it and those who are tired of being abused by powerful people, but resistance is part of the struggle to awakening and crossing the Graffiti Bridge. Crossing onto the bridge enlightened may mean confronting Spooky Electric in the violent room, but also outside our psyches among the people we are in relationship with. Even though there is a New Power Generation, there are still people organized to abuse power, and the temptations, even when we are New Power Generation people, will still be there.

"Release It" by The Time is about the power of ownership, the objectification of women, and the demands placed on women by men to engage in coerced sexual relations. The abuse of power is not just enacted by elected politicians on their constituents but also by common thugs possessed by greed and ignorance. In paradise, greed and ignorance will not exist. "The Question of U" seems to be about the conundrum between sexual gratification and awakening through loving sexual gratification, but Prince writes that all of his questions will be answered when he decides which road to choose, not knowing if he wants to pay the cost of selling his soul. Being here today means being in an existence replete with forks in the road, or many forks in many roads, where we can sell our souls, pay the costs, awaken to the consequences of our actions, and decide again. In the moments of reflection, we are waking up to the opportunity that there are bridges to cross—one of them being what he called the Graffiti Bridge.

After Prince contemplatively discerns his life's ultimate choices, which is what it means to productively use the fact of "being here," he has a spiritual awakening in "Elephants and Flowers." "Elephants and Flowers" is about a young man looking for a funky good time who is actually disoriented about what he's really looking for and what really matters. He realizes what he's really looking for is an angel (in the movie, it is Aura) and the savior. The song's title is his testament to accepting that God creates everything big (elephants) and small (flowers). With that understanding of God's reality in totality, Prince sings we should all "strip down."

Stripping down is a double entendre meant to suggest that we should become free of artifice and pretension. When we are naked, we are in a better position to love God, and when we do, being here now means we will live in clarity, joy, peace, courage, good health, and freedom, but . . . we have to awaken to the truth, over and over again and be willing to cross the bridge. But even when we are willing, there will be another obstacle to overcome, followed by another one. Depending on how long we live, the obstacles will keep coming.

In "Round and Round," Prince and Tevin Campbell sing about not really knowing reality or how to access it. We do many things to know, or fool ourselves into believing we know, but we talk and dream, talk and dream, resulting in just cycles of sounds and fantasies. These unproductive actions perpetuate round and round samsara (cycle of suffering) and thus block our ability to awaken in the here and now.

After "Round and Round," listeners are brought into master funkster George Clinton's (with Prince) song "We Can Funk." They try to make a case for enacting raw sexuality as a *Kama Sutra* practice, and they use, quite unfortunately, the simile of testing positive (presumably like testing positive for AIDS) for the funk in everyone's sexual fluids. The year was 1990 and society was still in a hysteria about gay men and communicable diseases. Still, "testing positive" was an ill choice of words because no one I know wants to test positive for AIDS or any communicable disease that inhibits one's freedom. "We Can Funk" is another opportunity to go back to sleep after awakening and delay crossing the bridge. It is not easy to stay awake to cross the bridge, but there are spiritual practices we can engage in to keep the hope that we can overcome, enlivened by the Holy Spirit.

In "Joy in Repetition," the singer has entered into what sounds like a typical (round and round) club experience, but an encounter with a sexually enchanting female angel seems to put a spell on her would-be lover when she repeatedly says to him, "Love me." Under the spell of the angel, his sexual attraction becomes imbued with agape love. This is another example of how the *Kama Sutra* influenced Prince's theology and music. Prince's character The Kid has no idea that the angel will be his guide to crossing Graffiti Bridge (for at this moment, he knows nothing about it), but being here means there are angels (or heavenly beings among us) and that if we pay attention and strip down in the figurative sense, we will be able to live with more resilience in the face of existential threats and the ultimate destruction to come. However, living with more resilience doesn't mean the end of temptation; on the contrary, it seems like the more we become resilient, the more life and its confusion is thrown our way.

"Love Machine," by The Time, is another song about the round and round samsaric cycle of awakening and falling back asleep into debauchery. It is a song about a man, or seventeen men, or one man as prodigious as seventeen men, promising to sexually fulfill a woman beyond her previous experiences and beyond what any one other man might do. "Love Machine" represents the men's sexual desire toward the angel while the angel cleverly uses the men's exploitative attempts to eventually lead them onto Graffiti Bridge. There is a saying in Buddhism that one should try to turn poison into medicine, like in homeopathy. Being a love machine can mean turning sexual desire into agape love; this is an opportunity that presents itself countless times throughout our lives. Should we choose the fork in the road toward becoming an agape love machine, we will have crossed the bridge through awakening, but . . . there will always be temptation and we can backtrack across the bridge as if we are sleepwalking backward as in the song "Tick, Tick, Bang."

In this album, Prince is rarely far away from the *Dirty Mind* persona that helped him rise to the top of the charts. "Tick, Tick, Bang" is about prematurely ejaculating a copious amount of sperm. Gratuitous debauchery? Maybe that is the real point. The more we awaken and reflect on our lives, the closer we get onto the bridge. Even when we cross it, life presents opportunities for us to go even lower into temptation's abyss until we completely surrender as in the song "Thieves in the Temple," where the preacher in the temple is nearly at his wit's end. He is undeniably vulnerable and can do nothing without the protection of God's love. He implores and begs to be saved from death, and, unlike in other songs about cars, tubs, a castle, and a hotel lobby, he is unable to turn this den of thieves temple into anything salvific. He admits his powerlessness—that in and of itself is a wakeup call. Was that Prince's greatest fear at that time in his life? The loss of being able to transmute evil energy into love? I think that was Prince's greatest fear for humanity: Despite our attempts to wake up when we are here today, we fall into temptation tomorrow. Round and round we go, talking and dreaming, making sounds and dreams, again and again, maybe even impacting and distorting our personality formation.

"The Latest Fashion" by Prince and The Time is a song about narcissism, retaliation, and lying to a woman for sexual gratification by telling her what society has come to understand what insecure women need—to be told how sexually appealing she is, even if it isn't true. It's funny how this song is called "The Latest Fashion" when men lying to women to get sex is probably as old as the "oldest profession"—the sex trade. I appreciate the place this song takes on the album, after hope; resisting the abuse of power; being in spiritual discernment; accepting God's power as the ultimate creator;

the rounds of suffering, debauchery, meeting and being taken by an angel; and then falling back asleep into misogyny.

Enter "Melody Cool," the character played by the gospel, R&B, and pop great Mavis Staples. Melody Cool, like The Kid, Morris Day, and George Clinton, owns one of the buildings in the neighborhood of nightclubs, but her building is a church. She sings about having been through it all, awakening, and crossing every bridge before her, qualifying her to be a counselor to the foolish. Whenever she speaks truths, the choir affirms with church shouts encouraging her to keep preaching the truth. She channels the creator God with a modern God-to-Job (the obedient yet long-suffering disciple of God) message to the people. Melody Cool is like an angel and prophet wrapped in one authoritative witness—especially if you're familiar with the real Mavis Staples, a Black Christian and gospel artist who crossed over to R&B and pop with her family group, The Staple Singers. Mavis Staples as Melody Cool in the *Graffiti Bridge* movie, as well as the Afro-futuristic funkster George Clinton as the embodiment of wildness, were important casting choices to make The Great Controversy case, through cinema and song, that there is good and bad, holy and sinful. Mavis Staples as Melody Cool is the town crier offering the clarion call to the Seven Corners, a lyrical bridge onto the Graffiti Bridge, that connects wisdom with devotion. In Prince's theology, wisdom without devotion is not the kind of love that will get anyone across the bridge into eternal life. What else is needed?

In "Still Would Stand All Time," we hear Prince's declaration of devotion. Prince finally, after all his trials and tribulations, being here today and trying to be here forever, awakening from ignorance over and over again despite the many temptations (especially sexual) that keep him in the rounds and rounds of samsaric suffering, and attempting to take the forks in the roads that might lead to the Graffiti Bridge, his surrender in the temple finally reveals that our glory days are closer than we think. He returns to the hope the album begins with. He still has the feeling he had at the beginning of the album, but the feeling is more intense, his conviction more unwavering, and his commitment to convince his listeners more urgent because he has experienced something—proximity to salvation—although he had not yet experienced death. More than ever before, he's ready to cross the bridge of many colors, peace, justice-making, and love.

The *Graffiti Bridge* trilogy is about the desire to believe in something like heaven, love, the perfect one—an omnipotent God—and a future worth preparing for. Prince sings that he's a witness, but he's more like a prophet letting his listeners and viewers know that the future is brighter than they think it is. How would he know? His belief in God and Jesus is expressed in the last song on the album, "New Power Generation, Pt. 2," a song about surviving the vicissitudes of life, maladaptive behaviors, addiction, and becoming strong because of his religious beliefs.

For the Dearly Beloveds who are gathered here today, we are gathered to learn what it means to be in human form. Throughout the lives of humanity, we will experience being knocked down, rejected, abused by powerful people, systems, and structures, sexual and racial objectification, hopelessness, separation, alienation, violence perpetrated on us and by us onto others, war, confusion between right and wrong, temptation, weakness, addiction, personality distortions, unethical behavior, and ignorance. There is also the possibility of cultivating resilience, feeling hopeful and joyful, and energized. Being creative, collaborating, learning how to be honest and receive truth, using power righteously, learning what true love is and how to live with true love in one's heart, learning what truly matters, and honoring the search for the sacred. Through experience and wisdom, we learn to renounce foolishness and futile attempts to change what is unchangeable. We are changeable. We cannot change God or God's plan. We do many things to know what isn't knowable, but even with futility in these attempts round and round talking and dreaming attempts, the reality of our collective, here today, but . . . demise continues.

Prince, I argue, was phallically empowered and inspired, especially as a "youngish buck" ten years after releasing *Dirty Mind*, perhaps caught in a bind I call the *Sex in the City* Conundrum, a phenomenon of staying stuck in a sexuality rut that makes it difficult to take life's vicissitudes while simultaneously growing older. I'll return to this concept later in the book. The preacher in the boudoir, without love, no matter what or how much he preaches, is vulnerable to evil and can do nothing without the protection of love. Melody Cool, the wise one who has seen it and done it all, witnesses the foolhardiness of two men representing two party clubs, chasing the same woman for the wrong reasons (but you have to see the movie to know this).

In Prince's belief system, being here today is an opportunity to be here tomorrow forever, never having to consider again what to do to exist, but . . . there is work to do in the meantime, and on that Prince and I agree. Beginning in childhood, as I already discussed, we are prepped to believe in things unseen, and explain material phenomena through magical and mythical consciousness. As a pastoral counselor, I try to pay very close attention to when my clients choose to believe in magic and myth over engaging in the uncomfortable work they must do to cross their bridges. I believe Prince's art, taken as a whole, is a prophetic tool to help us avoid the tendency to bypass the spiritual and psychological work necessary to make desired changes in our lives.

Can we be inspired by the ordinary acts of love, compassion, empathy, and skillful means rather than overly invest in magic, miracles, and myths to embrace the responsibility for doing the sometimes ego-crushing work necessary to make life more paradisical now? Yes we can and we do. It happens all of the time, all over the world, in a myriad of creative ways. It helps when the wise ones, represented by the character Melody Cool, played by Mavis Staples, testifies about her tribulations in the public square before harm happens. Mavis Staples of The Staples Singers sang in their crossover hit "I'll Take You There" that they would take us to a place where there is no suffering. Prince wanted to do the same thing. Casting Mavis Staples in this role was a brilliant move because she was a believable prophetic and pastoral authority pleading with her neighbors to bring an end to their feuding before tragedy struck. We can all take some inspiration from Mavis Staples.

The *Graffiti Bridge* Film

The *Graffiti Bridge* album, in my view, needs to be paired with watching the movie because the songs don't sequentially and thematically tell the gospel message to the uninitiated. Yes, there is trial and tribulation, sex, music, debauchery, wisdom, suffering, death, romance, an angel, and fear, but it coheres much better with the characters portrayed in the movie.

Between *Purple Rain* and *Graffiti Bridge* is the excellent 1987 concert film *Sign O' The Times* (presumably named after the 1800s Seventh-day Adventist publication *Sign of the Times*), which was co-directed by Prince, Albert Magnoli, and David Hogan; however, *Graffiti Bridge* was a real cinematic disappointment. It was met with almost unanimous critical rejection, even receiving five Golden Raspberry Awards, including Worst Picture, Worst Actor (Prince), Worst Screenplay (Prince), and Worst New Star (Ingrid Chavez). I must admit I am sympathetic with these Golden Raspberry Awards.

First, we have to recognize that the *Purple Rain* trilogy (song, album, movie) was such a colossal success, earning Prince an Emmy and an Oscar, that many an artist would think they could build on it. The problem was that Prince did not write, direct, or produce *Purple Rain* so the same success with *Graffiti Bridge* was unlikely to follow: Albert Magnoli directed *Purple Rain*. The screenwriter was William Blinn. The movie was produced by Robert Cavallo, Joseph Ruffalo, and Steven Fargnoli.

Nonetheless, *Graffiti Bridge* offers spiritual and ethical guidance, and the story is as good as many stories that have been told. *Graffiti Bridge* is a film about how we reconcile our internal and external warring natures and impulses to live in peace within ourselves, harmony and collaboration with our communities, and in accordance with God's love.

In the *Graffiti Bridge* story, there are four competing communities in an area called Seven Corners, perhaps representing the unity of the Trinity with the earth as described in the New Testament. Seven Corners is represented by three nightclubs and a church within close proximity. It is the angel Aura's principality. Morris and The Kid are 50–50 partners in the club The Kid runs, and Morris is in acquisition mode, employing a variety of strategies, including humiliation and violence, to take over all the clubs. The Kid's club (Glam Slam) promotes dance and sexualized spiritual awakening. Clinton's House represents hedonism; Morris Day's club (Pandemonium) represents greed; the Melody Cool club-church represents family, wisdom, and Christian devotion. The Kid, the main character, is profoundly lonely as a younger adult living with the fact that his father killed himself and his mother was committed to a mental health institution.

The Kid is visited in his dreams by a woman, but not the woman, his employee, who he's sleeping with. Morris is on his quest to own Glam Slam and consolidate the clubs. The club owners have their reasons to resist selling; The Kid's reason is his faith that all people, regardless of their identity, need a place where they can hear God's message of love and salvation, even when they are dancing or because they are dancing. The woman in The Kid's dream manifests in physical form, writes about love under Graffiti Bridge, and becomes the love and sex object of The Kid and Morris. Morris, who is in a sordid and exploitative sexual relationship with another woman, wants this new woman—for eye candy and sex; The Kid wants her for sex and love. The woman, sent by God, wants them to be better men and uses her sexuality to bring them into spiritual, self, and communal alignment by sacrificing her life because of their possessiveness.

Graffiti Bridge is about what it means to be here today. Being here today means being in a world that is largely unaffirming of our Dearly Belovedness. Throughout *Graffiti Bridge*, a feather (probably from a dove) falls from the sky. Aura, the angelic apparition-turned-real woman, keeps one of the feathers and twirls it in her fingers because the feather is a sign that God is real, that she became real for a divine purpose, and she is to remain on divine purpose even though she is engaging in acts that may appear sexually seductive. In Christianity, the dove is symbolic of God's peaceful and reconciling nature, so when the dove feather falls and Aura notices it, she is reminded of her purpose—to heal The Kid and Morris. (I believe the film is inspired, in part, by "When Doves Cry," even though this song is on the Purple Rain soundtrack. As *Graffiti Bridge* opens, there are two birds in a cage. I'm presuming these birds are doves because Prince kept doves in a similar cage in his Paisley Park home and studio and because of his hit "When Doves Cry.")

The Kid and Morris are imperfect, and Aura checks out both of their clubs, Glam Slam and Pandemonium, and laments what is going on in each place. In Glam Slam, The Kid sings "Elephants and Flowers," a song about the wonder of God's creation, but can't seem to help himself—he encourages his club customers to "strip down." Taken literally, they do strip from the neck to the waist, but maybe "strip down" really means to release ourselves from self-artifice. Nevertheless, Aura seems disappointed. On another occasion, when Morris and his crew are singing the danceable but comparatively vapid "Shake!," The Kid and his crew from Glam Slam try to impress Morris and his crew with another vapid but this time undisputedly pornographic song "Tick, Tick, Bang," a song about ejaculation and vaginal lubrication. Aura is obviously disgusted, and her disgust begins with The Kid and his crew's dance moves imitating sexual intercourse.

At Pandemonium, Morris and Jerome (Morris's employee and main sycophantic sidekick) get her drunk in preparation for the date rape of an angel. They walk her out while singing "Love Machine" to her and her responses do not reflect strong resistance—she's drunk. They get her back to Pandemonium, in Morris's apartment, and begin to kiss her until Prince arrives, blows out the lights, and takes her to his apartment at Glam Slam where he prepares to take advantage of her until he has second thoughts. Still, he engages in uninvited sexual touch by placing his body on top of hers before she awakens.

Dearly Beloveds here now deal with internal and external strife: There is chaos, represented by Pandemonium; debauchery, represented by Clinton's House; The Great Controversy and resolution of diametrically opposed values, represented by Glam Slam (and a phallic symbol); and Melody Cool's club church. When these values are near one another, whether intrapsychically or geographically, they will compete for space, presence, and survival. Throughout the movie, there are three phrases on the ticker-tape-like message screen: "It's just around the corner," "It'all come out in the wash," and "No One man will be ruler." What are the meanings within these piths and why have them spelled out and repeated?

Graffiti Bridge is an evangelical Christian gospel movie replete with obscure and coded religious references produced for a secular audience of Prince fans for whom most of the message would be lost without motivational and inspirational pith, in ticker-tape form, about how to be here now for the purpose of living forever in paradise. The term "graffiti bridge" means an inclusive reality that inspires hope and a crossing from this cold world to one where doves are cooing and not crying. "It's just around the corner" is encouragement to step onto Graffiti Bridge and take a step, then another, then another with a group of people doing the same thing. In so doing, we are here today as best as we can be. We are here, gathered with intention, to cross over from alienation to Paisley Park. Or, Paisley Park is the same thing as Graffiti Bridge, where the enlightened accompany those seeking encouragement and enlightenment to take that step into what is true. What is true? It requires faith in the saying, "It will all come out in the wash." Water cleanses and reveals what is.

Here Today, But . . .

We are here today, but there is no guarantee how long that will be nor do we always know what will end our existence as we know it. The "here today, but . . ." is the invitation and the opportunity to examine ourselves. *Graffiti Bridge* is, in part, about the yoga of merging with the sacred. Merging with the sacred is the answer to the "but . . ." that follows "here today." If the opportunity and invitation presented by the "but . . ." is accepted and worked, we will be here today and forever. According to Prince, this is what we're all looking for. In the reconciling song "Still Would Stand All Time," we see these themes that repeatedly appear, almost as mantras, throughout the movie:

> It's just around the corner. . . .
> No one man will be ruler. . . .
> Love can save us all. . . .
> All things will be fine. . . .

When contemplating what "here today, but . . ." means, the *Graffiti Bridge* soundtrack needs the story for a cohesive message about what it means to be provisionally here and how to use the "but . . ." as an invitation to pause, contemplate, and use a moment in one's life to prepare one's self for the afterworld. In "1999," he sings about Judgment Day and destruction. "Ronnie, Talk to Russia" is about nuclear annihilation. In "Revelation," he sings about the uselessness of the concept of time, which I take to mean the futility of trying to chronologically time the chronological end of time, yet the sign of the times in "The Love We Make" still indicates that it is the right time to religiously get it together, as in through Christianity.

There is a song on his *LOtUSLFLOW3R* album that I believe encapsulates what *Graffiti Bridge* is, and I love this song so much for its rock brilliance and message that I need to highlight it as a song about the practice of meditation and justice-making. This song should be played throughout the United States every time we celebrate Martin Luther King, Jr. Day. That song is "Dreamer."

Before listening to the song, pay attention to the art on the album cover. Prince's face is located in a lotus flower. The lotus flower represents awakening. There is a beam of energetic light flowing from his forehead or third eye upward or maybe it is being transmitted downward. My guess, given Prince's humility toward God, is that the beam is being transmitted downward, also as evidenced by the beam illuminating the circumference of the sphere Prince's face is in.

Now, listen to "Dreamer." He sings that after noticing how Black people are subjugated in the United States, he's "stayin' awake." "Wake up." "When I wake up." Prince, whose third eye is receiving a download in a sphere within a lotus flower, represents meditation. I wonder if this is what Prince was inviting his fans to do.

LOtUSFLOW3R (in a *Kama Sutra* artistic way of writing, Prince seems to be saying let us flow) screams or whispers "meditation" to me. The album was released in 2009 after he was baptized as a Jehovah's Witness, so as a meditator in Christian contemplative and Buddhist traditions, I wanted to know whether meditation practice was part of Jehovah's Witness practices and Seventh-day Adventist practices when Prince was alive. Meditation is practiced in these denominations. Meditation on God's words as expressed in the Bible are practices Prince may have engaged in or supported. In any case, I recommend listening to "Dreamer" for Prince's musical genius and his exhortation to awaken today, because we are here, but . . .

Practices

Being here today offers opportunities and challenges in countless present fleeting moments. Until we are made aware of how our minds are often caught up in memories of the past, fantasies, magical thinking, and fears about the future, we miss what is going on right now. Some people, when they are made aware of that fact, say that it is intentional that they do not pay attention to what is happening in their lives now because it is too painful or confounding. On one hand, they may be right in asserting their inability to handle what is right in front of them because this thing called life can be overwhelming. On the other hand, generally speaking, we can better prepare ourselves for noticing and accepting the facts, truth, and impact of our present situation, and mindfulness practices help.

Mindfulness means to bring one's sustained attention to something. There are countless things one can bring their attention to, but to use Prince's art as a guide for this thing called life, I invite you to first bring some sustained attention to yourself. It's relatively easy to do. First, can you bring attention to the fact that you're reading these words? If so, keep your attention on that experience until you realize that is what you're doing. Now that you've had that realization, bring your attention to the fact that you're reading these words while holding a book, reading a screen, listening to an audiobook, etc. After having done that and realized you've done it, you can move your attention to something else you are involved in. Try this mindfulness exercise while also noticing the words arising in your mind about your experience. Are those words generally affirming, judgmental, or convincing? The point is to notice if you're judging yourself or your experience. If you are, try not to heap more judgment on the judgment that's already there.

As I stated above, one can be mindful of many things, including how one's body is moving. When listening to Prince's music, pay attention to whether your body is moving and if so, how it is moving and how it is feeling. Try to notice without judging. See if you can practice mindful movement for an entire song, then reflect on the experience and ask yourself, "What did this song mean to my body?" One of the greatest gifts of sustained mindfulness is the cultivation of insight.

Insight

Insight means having a deeper understanding of something that is superficially understood, deriving meaning and wisdom from contemplation and reflection. For example, having practiced mindfulness of reading, and having sustained that attention long enough to be aware of the experience, one can follow that awareness with reflection and ask, "What does it mean for me to have been aware that I was reading those words?" Without forcing the experience, let the understanding(s) arise. See if you can mentally capture it in your memory. After having done so, see if your understanding has deepened. If it has, you may have insight into something you took for granted as true or was just a superficial engagement with phenomena. Can insight help us identify and transmute prejudices?

Prejudice means to pre-judge something or someone. Unfortunately, human beings are wired, it seems, to be prejudicial, in part because we are not wired early in life to see things as they are. Maybe we can't be taught to be unbiased at early ages. Nevertheless, the older we become, with wise parental figures and relatives invested in raising children geared toward differentiation, individuation, and actualization, our prejudices can be pointed out to us and our awareness can be guided toward realities that counter our prejudicial beliefs. Of course, our loved ones, when helping us broaden our horizons, should also help us tolerate our anxieties, but they won't be able to do that if they can't manage their own anxious presence.

Non-Anxious Presence

Prince, in public, exuded a non-anxious presence. He was the epitome of cool. He spoke about existential matters with a coolness, his voice was steady, low, and in interviews typically with few words spoken. I have no idea what was going on inside his head, but as a celebrity, he was often a non-anxious presence in interviews. In spiritual care, I learned the value of being a non-anxious presence for those with heavy hearts, living in fear, unable to make sense of their situation, and so on. When we are a non-anxious or cool presence for someone who needs to be seen and have their narrative received, the calmer we are, the less inclined we are to interrupt their sharing with something irrelevant from our lives, fidgeting, distraction, and other ways that signal we are not here today but we are gone to yesterday or tomorrow. Coolness like Prince exuded holds the potential to invite, with no additional words, revelations from others. When they are revealed, there is a greater chance that they will hear something that they had not given mindfulness to. Therefore, to be here today means they get to really know better what it really means to be here and what it means to be here today—right now.

Chanting and Kirtan

Please listen to "Purple Rain" *before proceeding with this practice.*

Chanting is a practice of repeating, almost like in the spirit of "Joy in Repetition," a short phrase that has spiritual meaning. I believe chanting "Purple Rain, Purple Rain" can produce spiritual meaning and invoke inspiration for knowing we are dear and beloved, gathering with the intention to be of benefit to others, learning how to be present for what is here today, getting through this thing called life, and so forth. What does the chant "Purple Rain, Purple Rain" mean?

The song "Purple Rain" begins with an apologetic acknowledgment that the spiritual friend's intention was not to cause harm but to see his friend experience joy. Then comes the refrain, followed by the aspiration to see this person completely immersed in joy. He continues to say that he wasn't trying to be a fling but a friend who was not possessive. Then comes the refrain, followed by the aspiration to see this person covered by joy. He offers this person guidance when there is confusion. Refrain and aspiration. The refrain is the chant and the chant is used to reify the aspiration, so when we chant "Purple Rain, Purple Rain," we commit and re-commit to relating to others with the heart of ahimsa (refraining from harming others), the desire to see them experience joy, to create the conditions for their freedom, and to commit or re-commit ourselves to the paths of liberation and wisdom. So, if need be, we can be guides if they lose their way. This chant can be used silently whenever we know we've hurt someone, are jealous, or are ready to engage in coercion, manipulation, and control. We can let this chant lead us back to the "Purple Rain" we want for others so that we may also bathe in it ourselves.

Prince was influenced throughout his career by a variety of genres. I haven't heard anyone describe his music as kirtan, chanting together in call and response, but arguably it can be used as kirtan. Prince wrote hundreds, maybe over a thousand songs that included forms of call and response to the lyrics of the truths he wanted underscored.

Forgiveness and Non-Attachment

Much has been said about the moral high ground and the efficacy of forgiveness, and the reality remains that forgiving is difficult to do. After decades and centuries of teachings about the need for forgiveness, I think there is still disagreement about what forgiveness is, when it should be offered, how, and why. I will not attempt to resolve this confusion and these dilemmas, but I would like to suggest that if we practice non-attachment throughout our lives, it might be easier to let go of resentment when it arises as well as toxicity when it remains present. How do we practice non-attachment when attachment is "wired" into our DNA?

It has been argued that our attachments, especially our over-attachments to things, people, our sense of self, etc., lead us to grief and despair when what we're attached to changes, disappears, and departs, especially when we weren't expecting it. Some say that our attachments as adults can be so strong that the experience convinces us, unconsciously, that the experience is a part of us, a part of our ego, and that is why it is so painful when separation occurs. Some say that non-attachment is an immature posture to avoid the pain that comes from commitment and loving others.

Here's what I think I know. Being here today, as fully as we can be, is aided by our consciousness not being constricted and distracted by our hurts, blames, and attempts at revenge. We should ask ourselves, "How important it is for me to be here today?" and if the answer is "important," then ask yourself, "If it is important for me to be here today, what is the cost to me and my loved ones when I spend so much time thinking about the past and wallowing in my pain?" or "What am I missing out on when I put so much attention on righting the wrong(s) done to me?" What is the return on your investments in thoughts about the past and future? If you're coming up empty-handed, maybe it is time to reorient your thoughts, begin reattaching to thoughts and behaviors that produce the experience of really feeling what it is and what it means to be here today, and live into those opportunities and potentials. When being here today feels like you're not living in the past pain and future revenge, forgiving will be so much easier because you've engaged in the "forgetting" that can lead to forgiveness. When I say "forget," I don't mean wiping memories away. I mean minimizing the impact of the wrongs so you can move forward to get through this thing called life without unnecessarily going crazy. Being Dearly Beloved means you deserve to move on from the past, but no one can make you be here today. Being a free Dearly Beloved means you can exercise agency to be free of those ties that bind you.

4

To Get Through This Thing

Listen Along

7
Diamonds and Pearls
Free
Paisley Park
Purple Rain
Sometimes It Snows in April

Being intentionally joyfully gathered makes it easier to get through this thing called life because we are reminded that getting through is not an individual task. It is so much easier to get through when you know it is your birthright to work it (life) through. But how do we get through? What meanings do we make as we're getting through? How do we know we've succeeded? Are any of our victories and failures permanent? What can we learn in the effort to get through?

Being called "Dearly Beloved" is a practice in compassion because we know getting through is arduous, painful, full of obstacles and temptations as well as possibly joyful and full of opportunities for connection and support. Maybe we have intergenerational connections that remind us of our purpose; however, even after we have gotten through, the time will come when life is through with us in the form we present with while we are here today.

It is a fiction to separate what it takes to "being gathered here today" from what it takes "to get through this thing called life." The whole life phenomena cannot be broken down into chapters. We cannot be here alone. All of life is beyond our comprehension. Loneliness is a threat to our well-being in many ways and getting through this thing that is beyond our comprehension, which depends on collective knowledge-making, is inescapable. In the West, we become deluded into thinking rugged individualism overcomes life's vicissitudes, we go round and round in samsaric suffering, we witness people struggling to get through, we read obituaries and attend funerals, and we know one day our time will be up.

Dearly Beloveds (that is all of us), those who are fortunate enough to be beneficially gathered early in life (unfortunately, that is not all of us) are better psychologically prepared to meet the challenges and responsibilities of their birthright to get through because they have experienced a form of gathering before they even knew they were a discrete entity—a person separate from their parental figure(s). Even if beneficial gathering was not a part of someone's early childhood, they can still experience gathering to get through this thing, but it may take practice in extraordinary extroversion to help step onto the Graffiti Bridge of non-prejudicial relationality. How did Prince see the challenges of getting through this thing and the responsibilities, especially when he espoused it was the end times?

Prince's Evolving Religious Faith

When Prince was young, he attended a Baptist church, a Methodist church camp, and a Seventh-day Adventist church. His parents were strict devout Seventh-day Adventists (although Mayte Garcia, his first wife, claimed his mother was Baptist). Gayle Chapman, a member of Prince's band, notes:

> Our first big break was as the support act on the Rick James tour. Rick would get his crew together backstage with booze and joints and they would chant, "Shit, Goddamn! Get off your ass and jam!" I said, "We should have own way of preparing." I suggested a prayer and Prince was OK with it. We'd hold hands and I'd say "Lord, thanks for keeping us focused. Let us go out and really stomp tonight in

the name of Jesus Christ. Amen." Pretty soon, Prince started leading the prayer. He was going on stage and singing about oral sex but he was acknowledging Jesus, too.

According to Garcia, before every New Power Generation performance and other Prince performances,

> We gathered in his dressing room to pray. No matter what else was happening, we came together and joined hands. He'd ask for God's hand on us, that He would give us strength and send angels to protect us from injury, that the Holy Spirit would lift up the music, that the audience would be blessed and happy and safe from harm.

In 1998, after the musician and Jehovah's Witness Larry Graham (formerly of Sly and the Family Stone and the founder of Graham Central Station) and his family moved to Minnesota at Prince's request to teach him about the Bible, Prince tour workers began distributing Jehovah's Witness literature before shows and Prince changed lyrics on previously released songs to conform with his new belief system. Graham recalled the following about his relationship with Prince:

> [Prince] sent me one of his new releases in the mail. In return, I sent a book called *You Can Live Forever in Paradise on earth*. He called me and asked if he

could make seven copies for the members of his band. I told him I'd bring him some books myself and we met up again in New York. . . .

Every night, after the shows we would get together and talk about the Bible. Just before the tour ended, he asked if I'd think about moving to Minnesota to continue teaching him the Bible.

We started off with one-on-one study. Then he came to Kingdom Hall, sometimes three times a week, for group discussions. The more knowledge you gain, the more you want to dedicate your life to Jehovah and that's what he did. Baptism is a public declaration of that. When Prince was baptized, I was with him. It was a joyous day.

The musician Wendy Melvoin asserts that when Prince was in his fifties, he had changed from someone who was excited to someone who had lost that excitement: he "shape-shifted into this completely different person who reads scripture and tells you fucking parables." The excitement about being a sexual liberator, even if he was still writing about sex, also waned. Alex Hahn notes:

> From the perspective of NPG [New Power Generation] keyboardist Tommy Barbarella, the continuing decline in Prince's work reflected an internal struggle between his desire to be a serious artist and his tendencies toward bacchanalian excess. "At the time I left the band, he was becoming a

vegetarian, and we started to have deeper conversations about spiritual issues. . . . But then he'd go upstairs and write a song called "Good Pussy."

Prince chose to get through this thing through baptism in the Jehovah's Witness faith. He remained an artist. On one hand, I do not share the frustration that he was writing "fucking parables" because writing parabolically is artistic, mysterious, and leaves interpretation and imagination to the recipients of the codes. On the other hand, some of Prince's coded language was very problematic—theologically.

So, we're left to ponder: was Prince's art really in decline or in transition to something his first fans didn't understand and appreciate as he was deepening his commitment to assist in helping us get through?

In "Free," Prince wrote about being vigilant and aware, yet confident because one always had the God-given freedom to exercise one's mind as conscience allowed. In his religious view at the time, liberty was at the core of his belief in God, so he could write about transcendence and prurience—and he did so for decades. Freedom, liberty, and conscience allow for agency—agency allows for being able to get through this thing. Providing comfort and counseling are also ways to get through this thing and providing comfort and counseling includes being able to accept that the nature of being human includes being internally conflicted.

Prince & The New Power Generation's song "7" is an homage to the destruction and salvation from destruction prophesied in the book of Revelation. Ultimately, getting through this thing means eliminating the thing that ends the thing we call life—death. According to Garcia, the certainty of Graham's Jehovah's Witness theology deeply influenced Prince so much that the conversations she used to have with him about spirituality became a source of tension:

> [W]henever I mentioned Akhenaten and Nefertiti, he explained to me how idolatrous and misguided they were. He kept encouraging me to hang out with Tina [Larry's wife], and I tried to participate in the study sessions, but it simply wasn't my truth. Men and women studied separately, and I believe faith should bring people together.

Graham mostly replaced Garcia as "the center of Prince's personal life." According to Garcia, Prince's hardening religious beliefs was a great threat to their marriage:

> He was hardcore into it and had gotten it in his head that God was displeased with the life he had lived when he was younger, and Amiir's [their son] death was part of the price he had to pay for that. He talked about David and Bathsheba and how David's sin had cost him the thing dearest to him, his son Absalom.

Even though Prince's religious beliefs became more systematized by his adherence to an inerrant understanding of the Bible, the lasting power of "Purple Rain" is an anthem about getting through by allowing (or adhering to) God's loving reign. Can you imagine if we all held the intention to refrain from hurting others? Holding the desire to see others experience joy while they are cloaked in the purple reign of love? Seeing each other as having the capability and capacity for renewal in constantly changing and challenging times? Committing to live our lives not just to satisfy our own desires but to help each other remain in the midst of the Purple Rain of love? This is how we support each other in getting through.

Practices

Appreciative and Transformative Listening— The Listening Up(ward) Practice

Please listen to the instrumental beginning of "Sometimes It Snows in April." Here are some guiding principles of the practice of Listening Up(ward).

1. When we listen, we engage in self-forgetting—it is a form of selflessness. Selflessness is cultivated by practices in lovingkindness, compassion, equanimity, and sympathetic joy. These practices help us locate our desires and attachments and help us soften the intentions to be immediately satiated.

2. When we engage in Listening Up(ward), we do so not to hear what we want to hear. When we hear what we don't want to hear, we refrain from convincing ourselves that we heard something else. We learn to abide with what is real. This learning is supported through practices in stilling the body and gentle breathwork.
3. By forming the intention to listen and be perceived as a listener, the person communicating has a better chance of experiencing a sense of being witnessed and belonging. The sense of being witnessed and belonging, if perceived by the listener, contributes to a projective feedback loop that supports the listener also feeling a sense of belonging.
4. Patience is involved in Listening Up(ward). Of course, we cannot listen to someone go on and on and on about the same things over and over again, but we can practice patience when we realize that we want something from the communication we're not getting, which takes us back to the second point. There is likely to be tension in Listening Up(ward). How to resolve it? Through mindfulness and skillful interruption.
5. Listening Up(ward) involves right speech, which may mean, paradoxically, no speech—no unnecessary interruptions and no imposition of our own story to minimize or maximize another's communication.
6. Listening Up(ward) is also paying attention to another's suffering, whether it is in the narrative, the body,

or a combination thereof. Spoken language and body language are not always immediately congruent. Practicing patience, allowing space for the congruence, often leads to clarity.

7. Listening Up(ward) also means practicing and using the fruits of practice—skillfulness to enhance one's ability to listen. Befriending silence, mindfulness, and meditation aids the ability to Listen Up(ward).
8. Listening Up(ward), as a practice, aids enlightenment. Enlightenment, in this context, means listening such that authenticity (through the upward and outward thrust from unconsciousness to consciousness) is revealed. The potential for witnessing a revelation can be transformative and diminish the impacts of a culture of delusion.

Redemption

We've all made mistakes. Some of the mistakes we have made have lasting impacts, impressions, wounds, and trauma on others. When Prince was young, he recorded music that was not entirely in line with his evolving spiritual and religious beliefs. Even if he wanted to erase those recordings from the face of the earth, he could not; however, as he grew older, he learned the value of love and serving others. Yet as a performer, he was caught in a conceptual and perceptual trap created when he was young, bolstered by the demands of his fans, and wrestled with the imprints of his youth while living as a senior citizen. Many heartaches and hardships are caused by our past behaviors, the meaning people have made of those experiences and that have been incorporated into their personalities, worldviews, opinions, and life choices over time. It should be humbling to be aware that there are people who are still hurting because of our interactions with them or our neglect of them in their time of need.

Can anything be done to rectify those wrongs? Yes. What? Accept the fact(s), reach back and out to apologize, engage in appreciative perceiving and Listening Up(ward) as described above, offer to make amends, and vow to live differently. Here's a simple way to engage in appreciative perceiving and Listening Up(ward) without following a formula. I believe every living being is unique. Every one of us is one of a kind. When we are gone, we will not return. Please try to avoid engaging in spiritual bypassing regarding this assertion. Don't try to deny the reality of each living being's specialness with the generalities of their species or the belief that they will appear the very same way they appear to you now and you will be in the same perspectival constitution you are in now. In the future, near and far, you will not perceive as you perceive today. You will not be perceived as you are perceived right now. To be here now means we see each other in our distinct moments that cannot be replicated. That's what makes being here now as we are the motivation for appreciative perceiving and Listening Up(ward). We can appreciate and perceive without agreeing with positions, opinions, behaviors, and so on. All we have to do is recognize the fleeting phenomenal moments of being or, at the very least, try.

Rising a New Myth from Ancient Forms

In "Diamonds and Pearls," Prince wrote to his darlin' beloveds about his proclamation that he would never abandon them, that love would reveal everything they had been looking for and would even heal their prejudices. When he wrote about diamonds and pearls in "International Lover," it was to seduce a woman to have sex with him. Prince, through the years, using the same words, could convey opposite meanings. Was he trying to redeem the lyrics of his earlier years? Can we practice redemption even if we have created a legacy of debauchery? Most certainly. As you contemplate whether redemption is a course you need to take, ask yourself if you are caught in a conceptual or perceptual bind that limits your authentic expressions and capacity for repair. If so, work toward breaking the chains that bind your healing capacities. Doing so will help you get through this thing with less blame and cleaner karma—a sort of blamelessness that doesn't give rise to legitimate causes for people negatively reacting to your behavior.

Equanimity Practice

Prince was famous, but that didn't mean he didn't suffer. Based on what is known about his death, we know he suffered; however, he attempted, as stated earlier, to be cool. Being cool is a hip or dope way of being equanimous. Prince, in his embodiment of The Great Controversy and his art, positioned opposites, like racial stereotypes vs. the wholeness of humanity; seeking pleasure vs. being of service; and objectification vs. relational subjectivity. He claimed being immersed in both sides of these "equations" and, in doing so, produced moral and ethical dilemmas in need of resolution. To get through this thing feels better when we have worked through these conflicts and have let go of beliefs, values, and behaviors that do not serve us and others. When we have done work to be more equanimous, we become the people on the Paisley Park seesaw with profound inner peace and, with that, a non-anxious presence for others.

There are many ways to commit to an equanimous life. Here are a few suggestions:

1. Reflect on what makes you so happy that you forget other emotions like sadness.
2. Reflect on what makes you so sad that you forget other emotions like joy.
3. Reflect on what it means to be forgetful. Try to see the value of understanding that just because you're happy doesn't mean that everyone should be, or is, and just because you're sad, everyone should be or is. The planet can hold all emotions, feelings, thoughts, cultures, birth, illness, aging, youth, death, health, and every gender expression without imploding. Sometimes, when my clients are stuck in a frame of mind that excludes the reality of others, I invite them to adopt an earth perspective—one that is able to hold different realities simultaneously.

4. The ability to hold different, even opposing views, simultaneously is aided by breathwork to calm the body. When the body/mind is calm, the impulse to attack beliefs and people who oppose our beliefs may diminish.
5. Any time the commitment to equanimity is present, one can also commit to humbling themselves by reminding themselves with this mantra: "I know a few things, but I don't know everything."
6. When in meditation, with eyes closed, imagine shifting your attention from one side of your body, then to the other side of your body, then to the top of your head, and then to the bottom of your feet. This is a way of noticing whether your internal energies are in balance. If they're not, and the desire to be equanimous remains, continue the practice of spreading the calming energy throughout the body while in meditation.

Mentorship

Prince's child was born with Pfeiffer syndrome and died six days after his birth in 1996. The bassist and Jehovah's Witness Larry Graham moved to Minnesota in 1998. Prince's first divorce was in 2000. He married again in 2001 in a Jehovah's Witness wedding. *The Rainbow Children* was released that year. He was baptized in 2003. He was divorced in 2007. As Prince's life illustrates, just because we invite a wise mentor into our lives doesn't mean the way we live will produce certain results. Nevertheless, when we see someone living as we would like to live and we believe they can teach us how to do it, seeking out a mentor can be a great way to get through this thing—especially if we think that is exactly what they're being successful at—getting through this thing.

5
Called Life

Listen Along

Darling Nikki
D.M.S.R.
Graffiti Bridge
Kiss
Pop Life
Ronnie, Talk to Russia
Sometimes It Snows in April
When Doves Cry

It is in our nature, as human beings, to name things. We call this thing that we are getting through *life*. Some other words that evoke life include *organic*, *process*, *reproductive*, *active*, and *growing*. This thing we call life is not easy to reduce to a word or words that convey the truth of existence, yet we contend with it as well as the anticipatory sorrows, terror, and grief of life's end. Here today, but . . . is a fair summation of this confounding and for some terrifying state of being, especially when we are taken to another world after our death.

Prince, from the beginning of his career, used ancient symbols (like the white-winged horse) that represented gods from around the world to depict otherworldliness and the power of the phallus. His most famous symbol, referred to as "The Artist Formerly Known as Prince," is a combination of an Egyptian ankh or the zodiac symbol for the Greek goddess Venus. I suspect that the phallic symbol representing the Greek god Mars that appeared on his Glam Slam club in *Graffiti Bridge*, and the many ways it has been depicted and embedded in other forms—especially his lyrics—found its way into the younger Prince's art as male-principled inspiration. If Prince saw himself as sharing the same mission as the Greek god Hermes or Daniel in the book of Daniel, with Hermes and Daniel being attachés between our earthly existence and "underworlds," then embedded in this ability to be an attaché is the archetypal transcendent phallic power that mediates life and death. Where did his belief in mediating other worlds come from?

Prince's first wife, Mayte Garcia, stated Prince believed he had met her in previous lifetimes. He told her that he believed in a soul and that the soul is born into the "same cycle" repeatedly. Was Prince influenced by Hinduism? In a 1996 interview with television journalist Bryant Gumbel, Prince shared that he believed in reincarnation. When Gumbel asked Prince about the child he and Garcia lost, Prince said:

> My obliqueness when people ask questions about that particular situation is that we both believe that thoughts and words can breed reality. How we look at the situation is very important. What we say about the situation is very important. All I can say is that we're both enlightened individuals that know that if you leave things in God's hands, you'll find out everything, the answer to the plan. So anything that happens, we accept.

This is another way of saying "It all comes out in the wash" as was flashed on the ticker-tape-like screen in the *Graffiti Bridge* movie.

Dear Beloveds. We are gathered here today to get through this thing called life. Our becoming is fraught and miraculous, but so is the becoming of other life forms. Other life forms support our becoming. Others compete against our becoming to support their own becoming, and some go in and out of support and negation, nurturance, and neglect.

This is happening all the time within and among countless life forms and a world so dynamic we cannot take it all in. Our becoming in this life includes being open to how life is, and that involves also being vigilant about threats. Opening and closing are part of life. According to Prince, there is the life we think we know and the life we should prepare to experience when the life as we know it comes to an end. Another way to frame Prince's beliefs about life and the afterlife might be: we know life on earth as largely a hell realm (boudoir, cesspool, den of iniquity), but should learn to discipline ourselves through love to be a part of an everlasting paradise we call heaven.

Hell on Earth

Prince's song "Pop Life" illustrates the hell realm that makes it difficult to live fully. It begins with the question, "What's the matter with your life?" then proceeds by suggesting it could be poverty, resentment, and jealousy, not getting what you want, preferring to look different, or feelings of emptiness, ignorance, and addiction. I'm sure this list is not meant to be exhaustive. Pop life is the culture that encourages filling emptiness, or flatness, with something that has no intrinsic beneficial value. Being impoverished can be popped with the pursuit of wealth. Blaming others for their success can be popped with pursuing success for ourselves to earn respect. The pursuit of feeding our every desire is pop life itself. Prince's understanding of the human condition was deep dissatisfaction with being ordinary people, being anonymous to most others, and therefore creating a spiritual vacuum that leaves us craving what we think famous or fabulous people have.

So, life on earth, given the human condition, is not as full as it could be because, by our very nature, we are consumed with filling the psychological emptiness with something that's going to make us feel more alive, powerful, excited, and deluded while simultaneously taking us down the "de-elevator"—not paradise on earth as Prince put it in "Let's Go Crazy." Nevertheless, we remain Dearly Beloveds even when in the throes of filling the emptiness—like Darling Nikki in the hotel lobby and kinky castle.

With life comes such a variety of mental illnesses and causes for those illnesses that it really does humanity a disservice to blame people for their illnesses, stigmatizing them and subjecting them to possible criminalization rather than treatment. For example, Prince's beloved "Darling Nikki" was just a character in a song that Prince was villainized for. To masturbate in public would very likely be considered a mental illness called exhibitionism. It might also be deemed a crime. Illness or crime, does it make the person less beloved? Both religious and secular societal norms expect us to control our sexual urges, appetites, and expressions. These norms define what is appropriate and with whom. One such norm is the idea that one shouldn't experience sexual pleasure from experiences of pain. At the time of writing, "kink" is a word used to describe sexuality that is not limited by societal conventions. But whether conventional or kink, when sex is used to fill a void, it is part of the pop life. Darling Nikki's castle replete with sex toys and a waiver of liability that her customer consents to might be the ultimate in pop life surrender—except when Darling Nikki is done, her customer begs for more and more of the sex grind.

More and more grind is a "round and round" samsaric cycle many people find themselves in when seeking relief from pain and suffering. We seek relief and satisfaction, but the success in attaining "satiation" can paradoxically cause feelings of emptiness and the need for more emptiness-causing substances to reduce pain, but not of the sadomasochistic sort. Drug addiction and consequent overdoses kill hundreds of thousands of people every year. Prince lamented about the pop life of everyone needing to fill their emptiness with excitement, but it is another thing entirely, an evil, when the pop within the pop life is caused by something called pain medicine that has created such a demand for the drugs that users die while trying to relieve their pain. The manufacturers of these drugs are being held to account by the survivors of the patients who died. Prince died of an accidental overdose of fentanyl. I don't know if Prince was addicted, but I believe from his music and his religious beliefs that he didn't want to be addicted. Addiction to drugs seems to be on the rise. One of the quintessential challenges of human life involves learning to say no in the presence of an overwhelming desire. Delayed gratification, or no gratification, is part of what it means to be able to "get through this thing called life," but getting through this thing is not guaranteed—just the opposite. Life is beyond our control. But, according to Prince, we need not despair but accept and be joyful that we have the opportunity to pursue paradise.

Threats to Our Planet

In "Ronnie, Talk to Russia," Prince puts a bop beat to the existential threat of nuclear annihilation. When listening to the song, one wants to tap their foot, snap their fingers, and get up on their feet to dance to the reality that we have the means to destroy ourselves—instantly and globally. We can advocate for a world of peace, but war is part of this life. Living, surviving, violence, and dying come with war and the threat of war, including the realities of climate change and catastrophe. No amount of pop fulfillment will change our true human nature nor prevent the humanitarian and environmental crises before us. I think we underestimate the connection between a pop-life mentality and the ways humans contribute to climate catastrophe. We've taken natural beauty for granted and we are witnesses to the extinction of various species—right before our very eyes. It is heartbreaking to see our own collective devastation of life on earth.

In 1992, I was driving from Indianapolis, Indiana, to one of the most beautiful cities in the United States, San Francisco, California, and I could not have been more thrilled. On the way, having driven through the flatlands of the Midwest in the dead of summer (with no air conditioning in my car), I finally entered Utah for the first time in my life and came upon Great Salt Lake. I had an oasis and mirage experience all in one! It was real, yet otherworldly in its majesty! It was so breathtaking that I had to pull over and get out of the car. The air was refreshing and pure compared to many places I had been. I was so taken by the scene that I began questioning my recent life choice to move to San Francisco, the city that represented beauty, but above all, liberation from all conventions, especially the midwestern conventions I had grown weary and resentful of. Given my goals at the time, living in Utah in 1992 did not represent the kind of liberation I was seeking, but the beauty of Great Salt Lake was tempting and stayed a part of my imagination for decades—that is until I heard that Great Salt Lake is evaporating. I couldn't believe it.

Scientists informed Salt Lake City residents that it was shrinking, but there were possibilities for mitigating future harm. Those warnings were largely ignored. Now, the receding Great Salt Lake is potentially poisonous. This situation brings to mind Prince's song "Round and Round," from *Graffiti Bridge* (movie and soundtrack) where Tevin Campbell asks if the truth is out there or within, where dreamers talk shit, in essence, in ways that don't effectuate change as they sit idly by as the world turns round and round. Is the victimization of climate catastrophe like living in a dramatic soap opera trap where we talk smack as lakes dry up and become cesspools and where we watch our non-human neighbors fall from the sky and wash ashore?

By a dramatic soap opera trap I mean, for example, we are making attempts to reduce carbon dioxide emissions through the use of electric cars, but the production of lithium batteries to energize vehicles to reduce carbon dioxide is depleting significant amounts of underground water sources. Round and round we go. So, should we just dance and have sex as Prince in "D.M.S.R." sang? The world, as he put it in "When Doves Cry," is so cold, must we just leave each other standing in it? If so, then standing in what? Constant conflict as represented by lovers who can't get along? But more than the conflictual couple in the song, Prince is pointing to the intergenerational "legacy burdens" of humanity as the psychologist Richard Schwartz put it in his book *No Bad Parts*—we act out the unbidden personalities, proclivities, and aims of our parents.

Part of the problem of life, conflict, war, and climate catastrophe is that we are inheriting and perpetuating issues that are not of our own making, that is, until we fall into the trap of unconsciously accepting our inheritances—whether they enrich or deplete us—and behaving in ways with others in which they are inclined to respond.

In "Sometimes It Snows in April" written by Prince, Lisa Coleman, and Wendy Melvoin, life is full of paradoxes: The afterlife can be better than the life we know, including the relationships we find there. Springtime brings expressions of romantic love, and also loss, fear and courage, abandonment, new discoveries, and thus snow in April. Contemplating this song, like many others, is contemplating the vicissitudes of life, and the song begins with a minute-plus-long tanpura drone-like quality to set the spiritual body for its life message.

Life is full of conflict. It's hard. To know one's belovedness and to be called into that understanding with the term of endearment, "Dearly Beloved," having been invited into an intentional gathering of how to recognize our tenderness, challenges, and demise, and those qualities in others can produce a profound hopelessness that actually makes a pop life a very attractive alternative, even though pop life strategies and implementations produce a deeper and deeper emptiness. This is where the preacher in the boudoir, den, and cesspool finds his strength: through the inspiration of what a gathering of Dearly Beloveds might find—the strength to survive these things in life, and life itself.

Life involves human-life cycle and personality development. The spiritual practice is to be intentional about our personality development. In Christianity, in Prince's reformist traditions, personality traits to develop can be found in Galatians 5:22:

> But the fruit of the Spirit is love, joy, peace, longsuffering, kindness, goodness, faithfulness, gentleness, self-control. Against such there is no law.

I believe it is incontrovertible that the fruit of Prince's spirituality expressed in his art is love. Looking back over the songs referenced in this book, there's hardly a song that isn't about love or the consequences that follow the absence of love. Another fruit of the spirit expressed in Prince's art is joy, and his dance songs were for moving joyfully even in the awareness of our impending doom.

In Buddhism, where I usually situate the core of my spiritual identity, there are also personality traits to develop, including generosity, morality, renunciation, insight, energy, patience, truthfulness, resolution, lovingkindness, and equanimity. Getting through this thing called life will present us with countless opportunities to develop ourselves into people who can be in healthy relationships with ourselves, but not just for ourselves. I believe it is this awareness, as we go and grow through the life cycles, that we see what we're capable of becoming and we will be willing to assist others in their life cycle journeys when they get stuck in past harms, traumas, fears, and self/other distortions.

Practices

Life Review

In end-of-life spiritual care, spiritual caregivers often use the practice of a life review, creating the conditions for the dying person to think about their life to make meaning, tell stories, re-author their narratives and, because they are still here today, take opportunities if possible to impact the meaning of their lives and engage with others they want to engage with—before they die. I believe Prince was right and wise to remind his fans that we are here today, but. . . . That "but" can be used to remind ourselves that we can engage in a life review even if we are not acutely dying. A life review can help orient and reorient ourselves toward what is most meaningful, the relationship repair work that needs to be done, and the plans that need to be implemented for the well-being of those in our care.

Genogram

One way to begin freeing ourselves of others' expectations is to chart the emotional and behavioral patterns of our families of origin. A tool for doing that is the genogram.

A genogram, developed by the psychiatrist Murray Bowen, is constructed horizontally and vertically for the purpose of creating a structure whereby emotional, relational, health, and cultural patterns passed down and inherited can be more easily plotted and revealed. For example, if known, one can put one's great-grandparents on one horizontal line, grandparents on the horizontal line below, parents on the horizontal line below that one, and then themselves and their siblings on the horizontal line underneath the parents. After making this horizontal chart, then horizontal, vertical, and diagonal lines can be drawn between relatives, connecting thoughts and behaviors they have in common. This exercise helps the genogram maker create a visual of the patterns handed down to them without permission and usually without knowledge, helping them to understand what their ancestors left them (the legacy burden) and see the opportunities for decisions they may need to make to experience the freedom to be who they truly are while remaining in an inescapable system of being. Being born into a matrix of human beings is part of life that is life-giving while also being life-challenging.

Genograms help us identify and trace the roots and trajectories of what we have inherited from others, including religious beliefs, likely going back centuries and geographies. We can use the genogram to reflect on what we've adopted, when, and what impact it had on us before we matured. We can detect a flavor of intergenerational transmission mapping, and its embedded prejudices, in Prince's art. I include it here to inspire you to look back on your history and what you were gifted.

In Prince's song "Family Name," from his pre-Jehovah's Witness baptism album, *The Rainbow Children*, Prince writes about the consequences of the enslavement of African people and the theft of their names. This song was written specifically for Black folks as evidenced by the lines where he invites listeners to choose a racial history and acknowledges that they chose African American. He proceeds to use the term "government name," which means the slave owner's family name the enslaved people were imposed with because they became the ill-gotten property of the slave owner. This theft resulted, for some, in intergenerational internalized colonialization, a distorted sense of self, belonging, and confusion. The family names Prince mentions in the song are Cah (the African), Lynch (the name forced onto Cah), Blackwell, Jefferson (as in Thomas), Rosenbloom, Pearlman, and Brown.

The way he writes about Rosenbloom and Pearlman leaves me feeling very uneasy. Of all the family names in the world, in the United States, why choose two names associated with Jewish people in proximity to the words about greed and evil? It really saddens me. I have moments of cognitive dissonance when I think about it. It makes my lips curl and my nostrils flare. I've been in this ethical quandary before.

Once, I researched the psychoanalytic Object Relations theorist I referenced earlier in the book, W. R. D. Fairbairn, who coined the term *internal saboteur*, because I was intrigued and impressed by his writings on the development of multiple egos and the ways we unconsciously sabotage our ability to love and attach to others. The deeper I got into the research, I learned that Fairbairn, the man who was the main conversation partner for my dissertation, wrote a policy paper recommending that gay men be forced into conversion therapy encampments! I was aghast! I asked myself whether I should reject his work as a whole and find another theorist to write about or expose this little-known policy proposal. I decided to continue my research, apply the theories that made sense to me, and also expose the policy proposal. Likewise, as much as it pains me to see this antisemitic swipe in Prince's lyrics, I strongly reject, as I do with Fairbairn's homophobia, that any group of people must be scapegoated and segregated to live our best lives, now or forever. I agree with Prince about what is instructive for Black folks is to know that the war on our sense of being is centuries old—and continues—and that sometimes we are complicit, unconsciously and consciously, in contributing to our own distorted self views. Using a genogram might help us begin to uncover the patterns of self-delusion.

Writing to Amplify the Literal and Create in the Spirit of the Holy

By now, it should be obvious that I value the practice of writing. When I think about "life" and the value of writing, I have learned through writing my spiritual autobiography as part of my dissertation that even though the facts of our stories don't change over time, the meaning and importance probably will. I have learned through Narrative Therapy by Michael White and David Epston the value of writing to the strong emotions within us that prevent us from moving forward in our lives. Prince was an extraordinarily prolific songwriter and wrote the *Graffiti Bridge* movie script; however, in this thing called life, we need not write much at all. We can write just a little at a time to discover and rediscover our lives, reauthor our narratives, if necessary and useful, and find the clarity and confidence to live out a new story since we are still here, trying to get through this thing we call life, with the multitude of challenges before us. I encourage everyone interested in cultivating resilience to get through this thing without succumbing to evil and be vigilant in our emotional and mental health so as not to unnecessarily go crazy and nuts, as Prince sang in his early career. I recommend two types of writing.

Keeping the young Prince in mind, when I think about his spiritual songs and the *Graffiti Bridge* movie, I think he was writing in the *spirit of* his faith and religion. After he embraced the Bible, the savior, and the prophets as the complete story and revelation, it seems to me that his music was more about amplifying the *literal*, not the spirit of. Both have their places.

Take a look at the literal facts of your story. What facts need to be re-spirited and amplified because you ignored them, for some reason, as irrelevant? Which facts need to be expounded upon because you sense there needs to be a narrative shift in the spirit of? Write them down and try not to edit yourself during the writing process. This is just for you as a reflection of your life you are a witness to. Once you've written some literal facts, ask yourself how those life events impacted your life cycle development. You may find deeper meaning in the facts you were already aware of, and this deeper meaning may contribute to new ways of interpreting your narrative.

6

Evil, Temptation, the Afterworld, and Going Crazy

Listen Along

1999
Anna Stesia
Annie Christian
Automatic
Delirious
Do It All Night
Free
Gett Off
Graffiti Bridge
Head

> International Lover
> I Wanna Be Your Lover
> I Would Die 4 U
> Lady Cab Driver
> Melody Cool
> Paisley Park
> Play in the Sunshine
> Private Joy
> Purple Rain
> Ronnie, Talk to Russia
> Sexuality
> Sister
> Temptation
> The Cross
> The Ladder
> Thieves in the Temple
> Tick, Tick, Bang

Influenced by reformist Christian traditions, Prince seemed to believe that Jesus would one day return to earth, the devout (the few Rainbow Children) would be awakened from the sleep of death, and countless evil people throughout all time would be destroyed. This belief is known as premillennialism. I grew up in a reforming Christian tradition, so I know the list of what is evil is long. I feel sad just thinking about the ways human beings who have created religions have decided who, beyond the what, are evil. I have counseled people in various religious traditions and people who do not adhere to any religious tradition and I've yet to meet someone who is innately evil, but that doesn't mean they believe they are innately good. Maybe Prince's Dearly Beloved salutation was not about one's innate goodness but about his fear that most of his fans, along with everyone else, would be obliterated in the apocalypse? What if underneath all the exhortations to lose one's mind, engage in sex without abandon, funk, and fuck all night long was a belief there was nothing a person could do to set their life right? What if being called Dearly Beloved was really about pity?

I sit with these questions because I feel that the younger Prince was more theologically liberal and progressive about the consequence of evil and thus more compassionate, but after decades of the wear and tear on his life, the compassion of his youth possibly turned to pity in his senior years. I don't know, but the role of evil and punishment sits heavy on this fan's heart.

Evil and Temptation

Prince's album *Controversy* is a good balance of songs about good and evil. It begins with the song "Controversy" (a nod to The Great Controversy concept in Seventh-day Adventism) wherein he chants the entire Lord's Prayer, which includes the plea to God to protect him from being led into the temptation to commit acts of evil. We already know that sex was his greatest temptation that he worked through with *Kama Sutra* theology until it no longer served him.

In "Annie Christian," he warns of the evil of being a false prophet. In "Controversy," he quotes the Christian "Our Father" prayer while also expressing a desire for everyone to be nude and a wish for no rules. In the opening scene of his 1990 movie *Graffiti Bridge*, the dance party evolves into a near orgy, but he's not in it. It makes sense here to state that "Controversy" was released in 1981: The first cases of AIDS started in 1981, "Temptation" on *Around the World in a Day* was released in 1985, and in 1987, Prince released the album *Sign O' The Times* with a song by the same title that indicated Prince was practically done with the artistic expression of imagining himself participating in an orgy—he was singing about the scourges of AIDS and drug addiction.

In *Graffiti Bridge*, he writes at his desk in his apartment while his sex partner is in bed, frustrated that he frequently has interests other than her. The next song on *Controversy* is "Sexuality," where he sings about the Second Coming of Jesus, which in his belief system means the world as we know it is coming to an end, so be free.

Are there limits to this freedom? In "Sister" from *Dirty Mind*, released in 1980, Prince sings about freedom expressed without the responsibility one should have toward protecting teenagers from incest with adults. This song is about the evils of incest and the sexual exploitation of a minor. Prince doesn't write that it is evil, but he fears being pimped by his sister. There is nothing redeeming about this song nor is there anything on the album that redeems the song. It is a song about evil, about what it is like to not be treated as a Dearly Beloved, with no seeming agency to remove himself from being groomed.

It may be the case that Prince offered redemption in his next album, *Controversy* (1981), where he appears on the cover as a preacher in the boudoirs he created in *Dirty Mind* (1980), *Prince* (1979), and *For You* (1978). The preacher, if there was one, was latent between 1978 and 1980, but emerged with gusto in 1981; evil was spelled out in "Annie Christian" as apostasy, vainglory (at the core of "Controversy") racism, murder, wonton sexuality (which includes incest, grooming, and pimping), assassination, lying, scandals, and the abuse of governmental power. The preacher who emerged from the boudoirs he created in the first part of his recording career became a defining voice and a legacy. For example, in "Thieves in the Temple" from *Graffiti Bridge* (the movie and the soundtrack), he wrote and performed about being in a place among people seeking to inflict pain. He is afraid he can't defend himself because these people don't fight fair and he begs God, the angel Aura, or the love they represent to make an appearance immediately because he is desperate for love's power to overcome his enemies in the crucible of the temple.

Prince realizes that he needs God's love as protection. In "Thieves in the Temple," he doesn't portray himself as someone willing to give in to sin. *Graffiti Bridge* was released in 1990 when Prince was in his early thirties, twelve years after releasing *For You*. He had gone through a developmental stage beyond the objectification of himself as a sex machine and sex object toward subjectivity with a mind toward what future generations should inherit from him. In 2004, when Prince was in his midforties, he stated:

> When you're a young man, you think you're the center of the universe. Later you see you're just part of it. The world is only going to get harder. Me and my crew, we love having conversations about music, but when we get deep, we talk about the future, about what we're leaving for the kids.

When he was in his twenties, he positioned himself somewhere between hippy and punk thought. In "All the Critics Love U in New York," he wrote that the hippy critics were not as appreciative of the power of sexuality. I think the hippies might have something to say about that. This is not the aspiration of the *Dirty Mind* Prince steeped in evil thoughts and behaviors. By the time he was in his midforties, he had met his spiritual mentor the bassist Larry Graham, been married twice, became a father of a son who died of Pfeiffer syndrome, and experienced the devastation of not having his fervent prayers met. Nevertheless, I believe Prince left for "the kids" potential-filled material beneficial for psycho-spiritual healing. Little evidence exists, however, to suggest Prince knew how his music could be used dialectically for psychological healing. Rather, Prince was on a religious mission—to prepare us for the imminent coming of Jesus.

The musician Lisa Coleman (of the musical duo Wendy and Lisa), a member of Prince & The Revolution claims:

> Prince would *never* mess around with the devil. That's for sure. He can talk God all night and day, but don't give that ol' devil a single *second* of your attention! So, the safest, and the danger-est, would have to be God. The God angle! Everyone knows something about it, so the demographic is perfect! . . . So there you have a culture of disaster obsession.

The disaster obsession was to be meted out on the evil ones, which, according to this theology, includes nearly everyone who has ever lived. As I stated earlier, Prince seemed cool in interviews, but this kind of theology tends to fuel existential angst, and if Prince himself felt that he was promoting sinfulness, how can that not add gas to the eternal flames?

In "Lady Cab Driver," a song about getting through this thing called life that includes evil, Prince writes about a lady, an angel, who has the power to transport him from his life of pain and confusion, not in a real cab, but in a celestial vehicle he calls a "cab," as in the "cab" Prince retreats to in the song "Annie Christian," (where he vows to remain until "Annie Christian, Annie Christ, is crucified"). He tells the angel about his fears, then surrenders to her evil commandeering while demanding that she drive Satan out of him.

Prince pays and repays the angel with sex. More importantly, his sexual aggression (sexual aggression to subdue his libidinal need) is met with her pleasure—Prince's way of driving the demons out of existence while also paying and repaying his female savior deity with forceful pelvic thrusts. When one reads the lyrics of the song found on the CD jacket cover, one will not find the "visceral lyrics" that are on the recording, where Lady Cab Driver and Prince are heard having sex—Lady Cab Driver having orgasms with each thrust and penetration. It is important to listen to each line to see how Prince is working through the sexual/spiritual dualisms. Here is a very brief summary: he gives a coital pelvic thrust for being financially exploited, jealousy, hatred, self-gratification, agape love, evil, confusion, appreciation, and more.

There are twenty reasons (not the twenty-three in "Gett Off" or the twenty-four of the sixty-four skills in the *Kama Sutra*) why Prince debases and loves Lady Cab Driver. When he's had his way with her, he has done away with the agony of The Great Controversy. The angel who rescues Prince from the troubled winds can handle all of it—all of Prince, sex with nondualistic intentions—bringing healing to Prince's troubled mind. He repays her with love, combating the forces of evil with the same kind of pelvic thrust yet with different intentions—the angel enjoys it all the same. This is certainly not Seventh-day Adventist theology and it is not *Kama Sutra* because the intention is not purely to cause the cab driver pleasure—it is Prince's budding nondualistic theology, sexual conventions be damned.

In "I Would Die 4 U," Prince sings, "And if you're evil I'll forgive you by and by." Those who have had a Christian faith and/or education know that unconditional forgiveness is within the power of Jesus or God to provide, and human beings are invited to attempt to follow this moral: "'Cause you, I would die for you, yeah." In Great Controversy thought, standing up and being a new breed leader for Jesus doesn't prevent someone from being killed and doesn't stop God's work of ending of resolving The Great Controversy, so why put one's life on the line in the name of God as Prince was trying to do? For him, to live in paradise forever was a promise too good to ignore and reject, but it took nearly a lifetime, in stages, for him to renounce extramarital sex, sexual objectification, orgies, etc. as evil.

It may at first seem difficult to understand what was going on in Prince's mind, but we can pause to ask ourselves some questions to gain more insight: What promises have been made to you that are too good to ignore and reject? Who made them? What was offered in exchange for you rebuking evil and renouncing a life of unholiness? How do you define evil, holiness, the divine, or innately good? Where did these definitions come from? What would help you to renounce evil intentions and actions? Has your understanding of who is innately evil tightened or loosened over the years? When I think about Prince's spiritual and religious evolution(s), I think about how he sought not to be reduced by the evil white supremacist capitalist thought to avoid being relegated to a "Black" category of art. Liberty of conscience is a core belief in Seventh-day Adventism, and Prince sought freedom from the evil of censorship and PMRC labeling that would have a chilling effect on artistic expression. He matured through the evil of sexual objectification, and he seemed to never waver from advocating for racial justice to combat the evils of racial prejudice, discrimination, and violence. Does your art, your life, address evil as you see it?

There Is an Afterworld

Dear tender and vulnerable beloveds, we are intentionally gathering here to learn how to make it through this arduous process, from conception to birth, to individuation, differentiation, and connection, through illness and violence, a sense of belonging and purpose, with a love for music, celebration, and pleasure that doesn't result in worsening our situation. Whatever we do or don't do though, we will die. We, in the physical form we are in, will all come to an end, maybe even a violent end that includes alienation from all that is good—including all that is included in the creative process many call God. Prince believed that there is life beyond our lived experience, so to get through this thing called life, we need to believe in life after life. That birth does not produce a birthright to this afterlife in the afterworld but to a conscious decision to not become a slave to desire. Did Prince, embodying the phallic principle and the archetypes of Hermes and Thoth, believe he was a conductor between this life and the afterlife? Through his art, it is reasonable to believe he believed he had a role—messiah, prophet, priest, prince, archangel, and conductor. What did his music indicate about his beliefs regarding the afterworld?

In *Doctrinal Discussions* and *Seventh-day Adventists Believe*, books about Seventh-day Adventist theology, the theology remained the same between the early 1960s and late 1980s. Moreover, if Prince believed in their end-days theology, then it is likely Prince held some belief that he and his followers may die a gruesome death. Ben Greenman, the author of *Dig If You Will the Picture: Funk, Sex, God and Genius in the Music of Prince*, thinks Prince, at least in the song "1999," is following the chronology of Ireland's seventeenth-century archbishop of Armagh, James Ussher. Ussher dated the earth's creation at around 4000 BCE. Drawing on the popular belief of the time that the planet would exist six thousand years and citing 2 Peter 3:8 that for God, a day is one thousand years, Ussher arrived at 2000 CE as the end of the earth.

The writer Touré, referencing "Purple Rain," asserts that the song was in part an attempt to position Prince as a Jesus figure:

> More than just loving God and making Jesus a central part of his music, Prince occasionally slips into wanting you to think of him as Jesus like. Actually, it is more than occasionally. Fans who paid close attention could feel Prince's winking acknowledgement that he was their savior and that he may have thought of himself as a Messiah.

According to Dez Dickerson, a member of The Revolution:

> There was a running subtext when I was in the band . . . a theme of "We were sent to help people see." . . . It was this sense that there was a certain enlightenment that he, and we, . . . were messengers of and we were there to bring this enlightenment to people who needed it.

Did Prince consider himself a prophet or the Messiah, or priest, prince, or conductor? Was he a priest or pied piper of the *Kama Sutra*? Dickerson claimed the band were:

> the messengers of some higher understanding in the guise of punk funk. . . . [Prince] had a sense of being called, if you will, of being a special messenger of some sort.

Prince, in the early 1980s, had a plan for a tour documentary called *The Second Coming* that never came to fruition, at least not as originally planned. Prince's *The Second Coming* concept had been morphed into the *Sign 'O' The Times* movie concept. In the song "Purple Rain," Prince sings about his ex-friend's desire for someone to believe in and follow, so he offers to guide them to the Purple Rain. But is the Purple Rain concept inspired by the purple robe Roman soldiers put on Jesus to mock his leadership among the powerless? Maybe. Maybe Purple Rain was like a "fucking parable" that frustrated his band members.

Maybe placing the purple robe onto Jesus as if he was powerless actually ignited and empowered Jesus and his followers? Maybe the Roman soldiers didn't know that they were coronating the new king? Maybe Jesus imbued power into a robe created for the weak as he imbued power into the oppressed people listening to his Sermon on the Mount? Maybe, maybe, maybe we can think creatively and have some theological imagination as Prince did, for the empowerment of the downtrodden. I think we can.

***

With songs like "Let's Go Crazy" and "1999," for example, we know Prince's message was an attempt to address the end-days prediction made by the prophet William Miller, the founder of the precursor to the Seventh-day Adventist Church. His belief, after studying the book of Daniel, was that 457 BCE was the time when the countdown for Jesus's Second Coming should begin, and 2,300 days or years from 457 BCE then would be the time of the advent, the following year after he predicted in 1843. Obviously, it did not happen, and the year was pushed back by other prophets to 2000. Nevertheless, Prince apparently thought it was his duty *as an artist* to help prepare his fans for the end times.
In Prince's 1987 song "Sign 'O' The Times," he sings about AIDS, drug addiction, and gang violence; between verses, he chants, "time" as if he is the world's timekeeper. Prince continues, singing about natural destruction on the planet and the scourge of poverty with misplaced technological priorities where women are faced with killing their children

rather than watching them starve while the government funds astronauts. The lamenting chant about time continues, but with a proviso of sorts—that despite impending doom, love and raising a family is still possible.

In *You Can Live Forever in Paradise on earth*, the book Larry Graham sent Prince:

> Although the first human couple disobeyed God, thus proving to be unfit to live forever, God's original purpose did not change. It must be fulfilled! (Isaiah 55:11). The Bible promises: "The righteous themselves will possess the earth, and they will reside forever upon it." (Psalm 37:29). (Revelation 21:3, 4 is also referenced.)

In "Anna Stesia," Prince implores God to help him attain his higher self—loving, wise, and devoted to Jesus. In "Play in the Sunshine," Prince sings about life after the Second Coming, that every day will be a holiday. Being in "Paisley Park" is like playing in the sunshine of living in paradise forever because it is all about everlasting love. Through an "Anna Stesia" pathway to "Paisley Park" to "Play in the Sunshine," one can also bear "The Cross" to achieve the same aim, or walk up "The Ladder."

Many Christians, like Prince, and people who do not identify as Christians but believe in life in other realms of existence believe in their hearts in an afterworld and believe that there is no guarantee they will be part of it. This uncertainty, I suspect, might keep us in prayer and supplication, and may also keep us believing that we are more than a physical being. We are also souls, invisible-to-the-naked-human-eye spiritual substances, that can be in relationship with God even after we die. The belief in an afterworld, maybe even a beforeworld as Prince once believed, is deep within many traditions throughout the world, before and after Christianity.

Is it only because we struggle with accepting our mortality that we believe in before or afterworlds? I don't think so. We have more stories of people having temporarily died and having been brought back to life and we have people taking therapeutic doses of psychedelics and telling their stories of past lives. Because young people remind us so much of our ancestors who they never met, because of our deep and abiding love to be with those we love, forever, dreams, UFO and UAP sightings, religion, culture, mystery, and because we are learning more about the cosmos and going to the edges of space and back, and telling those stories, I believe humanity as a whole will hold out the belief of other worlds and reunions with deceased loved ones. My hope is that people make a connection between their hopes to be in future worlds and treating themselves and others well in the here today world on Planet earth, in the Milky Way galaxy, so that no matter where we live, it will be a life worth living.

On Prince's self-titled 1979 album, he appears nude on the back cover, riding a winged, white horse (the wings of the horse block the view of his hips). Prince atop a white, winged horse may be his first archetypal expression. The author of the book of Revelation writes, "Now I saw heaven opened, and behold, a white horse. And He who sat on him *was* called Faithful and True, and in righteousness He judges and makes war." (Revelation 19:11 NKJV) The Jungian psychoanalyst Joseph L. Henderson argues that the winged horse is a composite of the gods Hermes (Egyptian; Greek) and Mercury (Roman). Prince, in the early stages of his recording career, began using ancient and contemporary symbols and archetypes to define, then break down, and re-design himself in ways that aligned with historic and collective symbolic and deific symbols. Combining these images with prophetic words, salutations of compassion, commitments to sacrifice himself for love, and pleas to his fans to turn toward God while we are here today, may have made Prince a prophet like no other. As you revisit his songs, treat yourself to his album covers to receive a more expansive palette of Prince the artist as he is known and as he was formerly known through his protest symbol combining female and male symbols.

Let's Go Crazy/Let's Get Nuts

In this thing we call life, there are the intentional choices we make to let loose, do whatever the hell we want, and go crazy, and there's also the stress of oncoming mental illnesses in need of treatment. What do we do? What happens to our souls, spirits, and psyches when all else has truly failed to provide contentment? What then? In "Let's Go Crazy," Prince writes a sermon for the beloved ones who have gathered together to learn how to deal with existential crises and divine promises. Prince told the comedian Chris Rock in an interview that he had to re-write words to the song because "you couldn't say 'God' on the radio. 'Let's go crazy' was God to me—stay happy, stay focused, and you can beat the de-elevator [Satan]." Opposite the cab cruible, the de-elevator (which is the opposite of the revelator) crucible is the vehicle for taking one to a place of suffering. There is no need to see Dr. Everything'll Be-Alright. With that as an assurance, why engage in the foolishness of medical care?

Prince, in this song, espoused that a doctor's pills don't compare to the healing the Second Coming will bring. We can presume, knowing Prince's spiritual upbringing, the coming is the coming of Christ, or, for the unfaithful, it's the coming of Dr. Everything'll-Be-Alright (the medical establishment) coming to hospitalize those looking, perhaps, for something that doesn't exist—represented in the song as the "purple banana." It is a sad and tragic irony that Prince died of an opioid overdose. In the end, he succumbed to a meta sense of Dr. Everything'll-Be-Alright, but that meta sense was lethally all wrong, as opioids killed more people in the United States in 2017 than AIDS and the Vietnam War. Prince was a victim of this Dr. Everything'll-Be-Alright street scourge. What's the answer? "Do It [sex] All Night" to get and maintain "head [an erection]" for as long as possible, be in orgasm all night as in "I Wanna Be Your Lover," and masturbate per "Private Joy?" That is an alternative.

In "Delirious," Prince proclaimed, as in other songs like "Automatic," "International Lover," and "Tick, Tick, Bang," he had so much sperm, it had to be released. Letting it go, being completely free to reject societal conformity, was part of the going crazy and getting nuts, the dance, sex, and romance that we might as well be engaged in all day and night long because there was no reason to not have a party and maybe even an orgy in the face of The Great Controversy's final Armageddon stage. The let's-go-crazy-nuts sentiment is not just about what to do, or not, as the world is coming to an end. It's about letting go of the delusion humans have that we can resolve The Great Controversy. In the meantime, is there a way we can be free and responsibly relational?

Prince sang in "Free" to never allow one's self to be controlled by the evil that can arise from loneliness. To be free, as it relates to the evils we face trying to get through this thing called life, we also need to act responsibly with our freedom. Prince, in his early music, obviously struggled with the tension between free thought, free artistic expression, and responsibly making those free expressions as they related to sex and sexuality. The Purple Rain trilogy's success attracted attention to "Darling Nikki" and led to the creation of the Parents Music Resource Center (PMRC), but before that, he had gotten away with *For You*, *Prince*, *Dirty Mind*, and *Controversy*. Me, my college friend Debbie, and tens of thousands (if not more) of Prince's fans were consuming this music when we were teenagers. Were we ruined? Should Prince have been renouncing evil as he understood it rather than propagating it? Here's the deal: Prince did what he did, made some attempts at redemption, and died in 2016. We should ask ourselves what it will take to stop trying to control others when we are not investing in controlling our own worst impulses. Let me go from the abstract to the concrete.

In 2023, a white heterosexual married couple became a news item when the husband was accused of rape by a woman he and his wife were having sex with. The wife is one of the founders of Moms for Liberty, a group responsible for limiting access to books on race, history, gender, and sexuality in public schools. Ménage et trois are not uncommon sexual practices, but the man in this couple, at the time of writing, is the head of the Republican Party in Florida. The Florida Republican Party, at the time of writing, is known for supporting new laws to limit free speech about the history of slavery, abortion, and transgender care for minors. This couple is an example of people not controlling their worst impulses, yet supporting laws that others should march to when they are unwilling to do the same. It is the hypocrisy of the ruling class that Prince railed against. Why do we project evil intentions onto others rather than renounce the evils that tempt us to blame others for our miseries and punish them harshly? Objectification.

Countless evils are done because we objectify. We objectify because in those moments of delusion, we aren't in touch with our true nature nor the nature of others. Because we aren't in touch with our true nature, we create illusions of superiority and delusions of inferiority. We create hierarchies, castes, classes, categories, races, and genders, and we create societies, policies, laws, law enforcement, wars, and so on to maintain these structures of separation. Sometimes, people justify these structures on religious grounds, and sometimes, people rebel. Rebellions are met with backlashes and the cycles of suffering continue. Objectification is a flaw that can result in evil and that is why those who are objectified must be responsible for their own non-objectification. By that I mean, resisting the pull to identify with others' projective objectifications of us. I believe Prince's life's journey as an artist demonstrates the power of not identifying with another's projections of who they think we should be.

At the beginning of Prince's recording career, his music was played on "Black" radio stations, but he told his listeners that he did not want to be limited by white supremacist society's notions of what it meant to be Black. In short, he rebelled very early on against being objectified. He was able to do this because he felt free enough (possessing liberty of conscience) to exercise agency—the power to be and express. When we feel others are stereotyping or pigeonholing us into something we are not, if it matters to us, we should use our power to be and express who we are. Feeling into our power can be done through mindfulness of the body and our thoughts; how we express who we are can be done on a case-by-case basis. One thing I feel I know for sure is that it may take a moment before we become real to ourselves and others, so being patient and persistent are qualities we may need to bring to bear before the revelation of our truths becomes manifest. When that happens, I hope you'll look back and say that the sacrifice to slow down and be honest was worth it, even if in the end, others hold fast to their objectification. The bottom line is, to reduce the impacts of evil, each and every one of us must stand in our truth lest we let others convincingly tell us who we are and what we're capable and incapable of. One truth about humanity is that when we are alive, there is movement within us. If we are able, we use our agency to make motions and move. We move for many reasons, and we move rhythmically.

Sacred Dance

Prince made music for us to dance to. He also made music for us to strip down and have sex to. His music was for funking and for f-ing, and it was not always clear which song was for what purpose and which songs were for both. Nevertheless, it would be an egregious oversight not to mention that Prince's music could be used as sacred dance music. How? To answer this question, I referred back to an article written by Rev. Dr. Alisha Tatem Wimbush, an artist, Baptist minister, and pastoral theologian. In her *Theology of Prince Journal* article "Dancing Before the Prince of Peace to the Sound of Prince: Working Toward the Integration of Spirituality and Sexuality within a Worshipping Community," Wimbush explained that despite some Christians' aversion to Prince while she was growing up, there is nothing in the New Testament to support an outright rejection of dancing, and within the Tanak, the Hebrew Bible, or Old Testament, there are many examples that encourage dance.

Wimbush offers a view that one's understanding of Christianity is impacted by the culture they are a part of (and I would argue, intergenerationally inherits), and the culture she grew up in included the intergenerational transmission of the culture of the Roman empire and its mind-body-soul dualisms or "trilisms," which resulted in dance being disparaged as uncivilized. Wimbush argues that this split can be healed by gaining an understanding of liturgical dance.

To arrive at an understanding of liturgical dance, Wimbush invokes the work of the Urban Bush Women dancers, who are "working out" their embodied religious and spiritual questions and concerns from toe to head and head to toe. The "working out" leads to greater integration and wholeness (a Christian aim), or the resolution of the dualistic splits. Wimbush uses Prince's "Anna Stesia" as an example of how Prince's music can become support for liturgical dance.

In the song, Prince repeatedly implores Anna Stesia. Who is Anna Stesia? The one who can liberate his mind from loneliness and duality, show him how to really love others, merge with the divine, receive Jesus's forgiveness and salvation, and be obedient toward God's rule. His way of allowing Anna Stesia to do all of these liberatory acts is through dance. Wimbush, as an artist, a liturgical dancer, and an instructor, believes that what takes a liturgical dance from being just a nice performative addition to a worship service and into a healing ministry for wholeness is its depth, authenticity, and relevancy to people's lived experiences. If the song being danced to touches on raw emotions, then those emotions should come out in the dance, even and especially in worship, where merging with the sacred, like Prince dancing to merge with Anna Stesia, is the liberatory practice.

As a pastoral counselor, especially one who has served in a mental health treatment organization, and as a person who knows many people who have struggled, taken medicine, engaged in a variety of psychotherapeutic modalities, and experienced improvement in their well-being, I take umbrage with the suggestion that mental healthcare as a whole, as represented by Dr. Everything'll-Be-Alright, is futile. I also take umbrage with the idea of going crazy and getting nuts in the face of the climate catastrophe, which requires serious responses from us. It may be the case that now, more than ever, we need to be sober in every meaning of the word, accept the harm we've done, and step into the opportunity to mitigate additional and irreversible planetary wounding.

Prince's art can inspire us to be engaged in the work of mitigating harm. We can begin by reflecting on the tragedy of his death and continue to hold drug makers accountable. We can cultivate wisdom and combine that wisdom with devotion toward the creation and beauty of our world. We can be inspired by the song *"Ronnie, Talk to Russia"* as we push our elected leaders to be in dialogue with other commanders-in-chief ordering their troops to wreak destruction. We can choose to not be boxed in by other people's limits of who they think we are and what we're capable of. We can lead lives of appreciation for our differences and the incorporation of people from various cultures. We can advocate for racial justice. And we can move from objectification to real recognition and relationships. We can achieve all of this if we take the time to understand that Prince's body of work as a whole is about love, joy, and crossing Graffiti Bridge into everlasting paradise.

Practices

Prayer

Prayer is practiced in many spiritual and religious traditions. Sometimes, prayer is used to ward off, combat, renounce, refrain from, and be protected from evil and temptation. Prayer can be used to build confidence to withstand the challenges of being here today to get through this thing called life and avoid existence in an afterworld that punishes people for not avoiding evil. I say that prayer can also be used as an alternative to going crazy and getting nuts, and I believe Prince really believed this too. How can we pray as a resilience practice? So much goes into prayer for resilience that I offer to incorporate other practices into this prayer life with the hope that prayer transforms the pray-er to accept, with equanimity, life as it is rather than life as we want it to be.

Before getting into the words of the prayer, or the posture of prayer, I would like to offer that prayer be entered into mindfully. That is, with attention to one's thoughts, bodily sensations, and breath. When you are aware of one's mind and body, check your intentions and ask yourself, "Why am I about to enter into a state of prayer?" and, "To whom am

I praying?" Is it to get what you want? To appease the gods? Avoid temptation? Look good in God's eyes? Everyone prays for different reasons and to different spiritual beings. I'd like to offer another purpose for prayer—the transformation of our isolation, alienation, objectification, and abuse of others as well as the cultivation of a non-anxious presence and connection with "Creative Sources." You may call Creative Sources God, angels, deities, ancestors, etc. Here are some practices to begin or support your prayer life:

Begin by taking a quick assessment of your life and get in touch with the contents of your mind and sensations in your body. If you feel at ease, be at ease. If you're not at ease, take a deep inhalation through the nose and a slow exhalation through a small opening in your mouth, as if you're blowing through a straw, then bring mindfulness to your bodily sensations and thoughts. Use a mantra to help your mind settle. You can create your own mantra or seek one from your trusted spiritual guide. If you don't have a trusted spiritual guide, here's a mantra inspired by Prince: "Dearly Beloved."

Right Understanding

When your thoughts and body are as calm as they can be, you may assume the prayer pose you've become accustomed to—the one or ones that take you out of selfishness and self-centeredness—and brings you closer to "Creative Sources," or the names and words you use to describe the power(s) greater than yourself. Knowing that there is and are powers greater than yourself is key to a deep prayer life because of the acknowledgment that you, we, are not in control. Prayer is an act of humble submission and therefore coincides with another practice, Developing the Right Intention to Cultivate One's Personality (keeping Galatians 5:22 in mind about love, joy, peace, long-suffering, kindness, goodness, faithfulness, gentleness, self-control), and the Buddhist character perfections—generosity, morality, patience, lovingkindness, truthfulness, equanimity, insight, energy, resolve, and meditative concentration—in mind for inspiration, not religious adherence. A prayer for resilience is an antidote to an "Annie Christian" narcissism that takes from others that which wasn't freely given because of the delusion of entitlement. This is *Right Understanding*.

Wholesome Desire

In this state of prayer, nothing in particular is being asked for other than the encouragement to continue having a prayer life. What will follow from this practice is not known, so being open to mystery is important. Being open to accepting realities that were unacceptable before is possible. Slowing down is likely. Getting in touch with one's state of being is probable. Learning to be with people different from you is possible. Ultimately, a prayer to promote resilience can help us get through this thing for as long as we are a part of this thing. For these reasons, I say this is the cultivation of *wholesome desire*.

Humility

Whether you believe in other worlds, you would probably do well, and experience some peace of mind, to admit that you don't know and understand everything. All you have to do, on occasion, is remind yourself of this fact. When you remind yourself that you don't know everything, pause and bring your attention to your thoughts and bodily sensations. If you can accept, with ease, that you don't know everything, take your humility to another level. Remind yourself that you don't know most things. Pause, reflect, and settle. Once settled, remind yourself that you cannot know most things and see if you can feel into the release from the delusion you may have been carrying. Try to take a deep breath and bring a slight smile to your face. See if you can go about your day appreciating mystery. Last, ask yourself if you would be willing to contribute some goodness to the plane of existence you know you are a part of. Then—go forth and do it!

Sacred Dance

Inspired by Wimbush's understanding of liturgical dance, keeping "Anna Stesia" in mind, choose a Prince song about merging with the sacred. There are many such songs. Commit to practicing mindfulness of the body, including its internal movements of fluids, muscles, and organs. Recognize where you have embodied the blocks to your authenticity, where you harbor splits between mind, body, and soul or spirit as you understand them. Make it your intention to heal from these splits in order to experience wholeness and know true love. Play the music and move to the rhythm. No choreography, audience, or dance partner is needed. Listen, feel, move, release, heal, listen, feel, move, release, and heal. If joy arises, let it. If sorrow arises, let it.

Four Heavenly Abodes Centering Yoga Practice

As a pastoral counselor, I listen for my clients' areas of spiritual and emotional strengths. I listen for their capacities to love themselves and others, and I listen as they talk about their struggles to radically accept people as they are and rejoice in their particularities—especially when there are personality or ethical challenges. I'm curious about the resources they utilize when life is especially difficult. If what they have used in the past helps them live with more ease, I tend to remind them that they can still use that resource. If that resource is no longer effective or they want to try something different, I offer spiritual practices in lovingkindness meditation practice, examining one's thoughts and reframing negative thought patterns; mantras; extending the amount of time or frequency in prayer and meditation, including new prayers; removing one's self from harmful habits; and so on. One of the practices I created for cultivating darlin' Dearly Beloved consciousness is the Four Heavenly Abodes Centering Yoga practice. Please adapt it to your body and mind as is comfortable for you.

Sitting Posture

Sit in a half-lotus position, or another position that supports your being still, practicing mindfulness of the breath for about twenty to fifty minutes. Bring your hands into the Uttarabodhi mudra. In this mudra, the tips of your forefingers touch by bringing your right thumb to rest in the V formed by your outstretched left index finger and your left thumb; your left thumb is resting on the V of your right hand created by the outstretched index finger and thumb of your right hand. The rest of your fingers are intertwined—left middle finger on top of right middle finger, left ring finger on top of right ring finger, and left pinky on top of right pinky. Rest your forearms on your inner thighs with your palms facing upward. Remember to make whatever adjustments you need to make for the realities of your body parts and abilities.

Breath

Allow your breathing to be what it is, returning your attention to the sensations of breathing at the tip of your nostrils, after you notice your thoughts are making a story or recalling a memory.

Centering Words

After your allotted time has passed, bring a heavenly abode word to mind. So I avoid as much discursiveness as possible,

I usually begin with the word "lovingkindness," followed by "compassion," then "equanimity," then "sympathetic joy."

Invoking Sensations and Visualization
Lovingkindness

Bring the word "lovingkindness" to mind and center or rest with that word on your mind for a few seconds. Then, locate in your body where you feel lovingkindness. Wherever that is, imagine using your bodily energy to disperse the lovingkindness energy throughout your entire body. After you have visualized being immersed in lovingkindness, collapse the Uttarabodhi mudra and then bring your palms together in *gassho* or "respect"—prayer pose—with the sides of your thumbs at your sternum. By doing so, the feeling of lovingkindness often feels more intense, though there is no guarantee there will be any feeling. After a few seconds with your thumbs against your sternum, move the prayer mudra upward, gently pressing the side of your thumbs to your lips as a reminder to try to speak words of love and kindness. After resting the sides of your thumbs against your lips, bring the prayer mudra up to your forehead as a reminder to try to think loving and kind thoughts. After resting for a few seconds, bow, keep your prayer mudra to your head, and stay in a bowed position long enough to feel a surrender to the abode. When rising, still in your seated position, begin the sequence again with the word "compassion" and then center and rest before the visualization, the hands, and the bowing. Then, I start the sequence again with the word "equanimity."

You may incorporate the equanimity practice discussed earlier at this juncture in the practice. Unlike with the other two abodes, with equanimity, try to balance your energy side to side and up and down so that you feel a subtle solidity that supports your sitting posture and vice versa.

When I bring sympathetic joy to mind, I intentionally bring a slight smile to my face because I know that the power of an intentional smile on my body during meditation can alter my mood toward joy. Try to put a slight smile on your face no matter what you are feeling. Going through the affective valances of these abodes prepares you for your closing prayer.

Brief Closing Prayer

During my chaplaincy training, combined with my education at a Catholic university, I came to appreciate the Prayer of St. Francis:

> Lord, make me an instrument of your peace.
> Where there is hatred, let me bring love.
> Where there is offense, let me bring pardon.
> Where there is discord, let me bring union.
> Where there is error, let me bring truth.
> Where there is doubt, let me bring faith.
> Where there is despair, let me bring hope.
> Where there is darkness, let me bring your light.
> Where there is sadness, let me bring joy.
> O Master, let me not seek as much

> to be consoled as to console,
> to be understood as to understand,
> to be loved as to love,
> for it is in giving that one receives,
> it is in self-forgetting that one finds,
> it is in pardoning that one is pardoned,
> it is in dying that one is raised to eternal life.

I don't recite the entire prayer in my daily practice. I just center and rest on the phrase, "Make me an instrument of your peace" and the feeling of peace. Another word for peace is "equanimity"; through dialecticism (the interpenetration of opposites like hatred and love, offense and pardon, etc.), I experience balance. This ends my practice. What prayer will you choose to end your practice?

In the interest of being able to see everyone as darlin' Dearly Beloveds, reflect on the Prayer of St. Francis again. As we get through this thing called life, humans experience hatred, offense, discord, error, doubt, despair, darkness, and sadness. Sometimes, we are the perpetrators and, sometimes, the victim. Sometimes, we embody both. This thing called life is difficult for everyone, bar none, so practice addressing people through the vulnerability we all share. And when you do, people will come to know that they are your darlin' Dearly Beloveds.

7
Redemption and the Rising of the Rainbow Children

> **Listen Along**
>
> $
> 1999
> affirmation I & II
> affirmation III
> Alphabet St.
> Art Official Cage
> Eye No
> Family Name
> Forever in My Life
> Graffiti Bridge

> Lovesexy
> Muse 2 the Pharaoh
> One of Us
> Positivity
> Purple Rain
> Sex in the Summer
> Strange Relationship
> Temptation
> The Ballad of Dorothy Parker
> Holy River
> The Love We Make
> The Rainbow Children
> When 2 R in Love

Prince's Shifting Sexual Consciousness

Prince's earliest albums were full of songs about sexual temptation and giving in to those temptations. In "Soft and Wet" from his first album *I'm Yours*, released in 1978 when Prince was nineteen years old, he wrote that he wasn't interested in being righteous if being so meant he could not experience lust. These lyrics, I believe, exemplify the core of his "surrender to the sexual urge" message in his early recording; however, by 1988, when Prince was thirty, after *Prince, Dirty Mind, Controversy, Purple Rain*, and *Sign O' The Times* were released, he released *Lovesexy*. The lyrics from the nine songs, taken together, offer a different message about surrendering to sexual urges—there is a message of love throughout the album.

In "Eye No," he wrote that we all should heed love's call. In "Alphabet St.," he wrote a rap about the centrality of the love that needs to be "put down" when one feels insecurity, egotism, freakiness, and horniness. In "Glam Slam," he writes that being overcome with freaky lust is the same as love. In "Anna Stesia," he writes about learning to love. In "When 2 R in Love," he writes about sex as love when a couple whispers to each other, when they have butterflies in their stomachs, the impact of love on their ability to cognize reality, deep intimacy, shamelessness, and the excitement of anticipatory sex. It's mutual. In "I Wish U Heaven," he writes about his wish for his beloved to know love, then heaven, and in the refrain, love and heaven in a back-and-forth way. In "Positivity," he sings of love, harmony, and peace and he ends the song with an exhortation to avoid the beast (Spooky Electric). In addition to the warning, he calls on his backup singers, all the boys and girls, as the new kings of the world, as a heavenly court singing together to hold on to our souls. Prince is drawing explicitly on Christian evangelistic zeal.

Since sex without love in 1978 in his twenties seems to have transitioned to sex with love in his thirties in 1988, this made me revisit *Sign O' The Times* (released in 1987, the year before *Lovesexy*) to see if there was a hint that his understanding of the signs led him to write about sexuality in and as love. In "Play in the Sunshine," Prince wrote about unconditionally loving one's enemies until they can no longer resist and until they surrender to love. In "The Ballad of Dorothy Parker," Prince references Joni Mitchell's classic "Help Me" as Dorothy Parker's favorite song being played on the radio, but before Joni Mitchell is heard singing "in love with you," the phone rings. The absence of the love lyrics eventually leads Prince, in the song, to abandon his care for the woman he is dating and undress for Dorothy Parker. In "Slow Love," Prince wrote about being able to see the truth of the love in his lover's eyes. What I find beautiful about these lyrics is that before this song, Prince was not singing about looking into his lover's eyes for truth because his primary focus before then was the need for his own sexual release.

I believe "Forever in My Life" is the most obvious hint I was looking for—the shift in consciousness from the immature sex objectification of his twenties to valuing love with sex that led to *Lovesexy* and *Graffiti Bridge*. In "Forever in My Life," a maturing and more relationally oriented Prince wrote about the male life cycle where a man tires of the samara and emptiness of female sexual objectification and the surprising effect love has had on him to make him want to be attached in a monogamous relationship with someone he recognizes as having the capacity to truly respect him. He respects her in return, and this mutuality frees him to dream. Dream. Love, commitment, and attachment may have inspired Prince to be more like Daniel in the book of Daniel, the interpreter of dreams, and as it was once put, the creator of "fucking parables."

Prince also met Larry Graham, a Jehovah's Witness, in 1988. Prince was obviously impressed with his ability to play the bass, but was also impressed with Graham the man— Graham became Prince's spiritual mentor. About ten years later when Prince was thirty-eight or thirty-nine years old, two years before Graham moved to Minnesota to be closer to Prince, he released *Emancipation* (1996). What did it mean for Prince to be free? In this album, I looked for spiritual evolution from the sexual objectification and surrender to temptation expressed in his twenties to the incorporation of love in his thirties. What might be next and would it be expressed in *Emancipation*?

In "Sex in the Summer," he wrote about listening to "Mahalia" (presumably the iconic gospel singer Mahalia Jackson), reading Christian devotionals, his relationship with "Kirk" (presumably the contemporary gospel singer Kirk Franklin), and the value and promise of Christian faith to end suffering and illness. In "Sex in the Summer," Prince continues his merging of the profane and sacred.

However, in "The Holy River," Prince sings about himself and his lover being baptized, thereby ending sexual objectification, embracing monogamy, and religious devotion and praise. In "One of Us," written by Eric Bazilian, Prince asks if we would have the courage to change if we had the opportunity to see God. In "The Love We Make," Prince did not write about sex but about our responsibility to love one another as Jesus's Second Coming was fast approaching. Part of this love, in Prince's theology, includes the destruction of those who have harmed us. That promise is used as a way to help the downtrodden feel hopeful that those who harm us will be killed. Justice is an inevitability. Selfless prayer, gratitude, and love will be our protection. In "New World," Prince writes about facing difficult changes with love for one another. Those difficult changes include fluid gender expressions, invasion of privacy, medical technologies to reverse aging, altering personalities in the womb, and de-racializing people.

I found the maturing Prince of love I was looking for. It is as if Prince, the prophet, is telling his listeners that the dualities we have relied upon in the divided world humans created are vanishing and the only way we are going to survive this new world of less duality, and consequently more confusion, ignorance, and violence if we're not conscious and careful, is through love. The young Prince may have considered these changes as signs of impending doom, but the older Prince chose to publish lyrics about loving others—regardless—well, mostly. I think that was the evolution I anticipated.

The Rainbow Children

Based on *Sign O' The Times* (1987) and *Lovesexy* (1988), I argue that Prince was on a long and winding redemption road, not radical or perfect, but toward being loving. *Emancipation* (1996) was an extension of the redemption project; however, the album didn't go nearly as far as I expected it would go from a spiritual journeyperson and self-appointed leader in his forties. However, *The Rainbow Children* album (2001) far and away exceeded my expectations while also terribly troubling me because of the antisemitic slights.

The Rainbow Children was released when Prince was in his forties, about two years before he was baptized as a Jehovah's Witness. Like *Graffiti Bridge*, *The Rainbow Children* is not a Prince standard-style gospel offering. I don't need to forgive Prince for the album like I felt I needed to be forgiving of the roundly and rightly panned *Graffiti Bridge* movie because of its poor theatrical qualities, but I want to encourage readers to listen to *The Rainbow Children* a few times before assessing the quality of its gospel expression.

I, like millions of his fans, was habituated to a certain expectation of what Prince's music would sound like. After all, I was habituated to the younger Prince when I was about his age, stuck perhaps in my own expectations. When I first heard *The Rainbow Children*, I was confused. It begins with jazz. I love jazz, but I wasn't expecting jazz from Prince because it wasn't the funk, R&B, or rock I was accustomed to hearing from him.

In Arion Berger's 2002 review of *The Rainbow Children* in *Rolling Stone*, he wrote:

> It isn't expedience, it isn't desperation, it isn't eccentricity of vision per se: Whatever compels Prince to continue expounding on his idea of a spirito-sexual musical revolution remains a mystery all these records away from his greatest, most populist work. He's digging in his high heels harder than ever on the busy, portentous *The Rainbow Children*. It cops jazz forms without swinging, gets James Brownishly

funky minus the urgency, and offers church interludes that are too mystical to carry earthly convention. Laid out as a series of "chapters," the tracks provide a text for the everywhereness of God and find him mostly in the bedroom. Heavily processed vocal intros provide a biblical weight to each number, as do Gnostic references to the Banished Ones, ambiguous numerology, ambiguous vegetarianism and his talk of "displaced bloodlines." But this is Prince, and if the laid-back jazz funk doesn't interest him, he can always get rowdy with the ladies. His admonishing tone and dubious history take a back seat to the fine, sexy stuff—the simple ballad "She Loves Me 4 Me," the grooving "Mellow" and "1 + 1 + 1 = 3." But it's a long trudge across the desert to this heady water, especially with Freak-in-the-Pulpit leading the way, waving his synthesizer of holy justice.

I sympathize and agree with Berger's review as someone habituated by Prince's earliest recordings. I'm also impressed he referred to Prince as the "Freak-in-the-Pulpit." Berger meant "freak" in the sexual way—I could not agree more. I also sympathize and agree with reviewer Andy Healy on the Albumism website. He concluded his 2021 (a nineteen-year retrospective) review with this paragraph:

> *The Rainbow Children* remains a deliberately confronting album, and its highly religious narrative

might be too much for some. As a whole, it can be a lot to get through, but it contains some unforgettable moments of a man renewed by a reclaimed identity and the freedom to go where the muse takes him. It's a shame that most people exposed to Prince's most popular recordings missed out on some of his most powerful in the later efforts, but this was not destined to be the album that would bring them back.

Agreed. I don't think *The Rainbow Children* should be the album that brings fans to his later works. Why not? Here's my 2024 review:

The Rainbow Children is a multi-genre gospel album of hope that is also highly problematic. It's surprising, irritating, confusing, and destructive. Therefore, a few contemplative listens (if possible) need to take place to begin to put the puzzle pieces together. Unlike many recordings today, it is actually an album, one that tells a larger story with a beginning, arc, and ending that is somewhat coherent, but in places offers an awful message.

The album begins with the once familiar, slowed down deep bass voice of God that we heard in 1982 in "1999" saying, "Don't worry, I won't hurt you, I only want you to have some fun." What is God's voice saying in "The Rainbow Children?" Human beings who really understand God and God's laws are building a new nation, and those people are the Rainbow Children. Anticipating that his listeners expect to hear rock and funk, Prince interjects jazz into his gospel.

Surprise! It is important to understand that the Rainbow Children are dead while awaiting the Second Coming of Jesus. Also, we are re-introduced to the chant "Reproduction of a new breed leaders, stand up, organize." Sound familiar? This chant is from 1981 in "Sexuality," but what is being stood up for in the "Rainbow Children" is not sexuality but Christian nation-building, where non-Christians will surely be discriminated against. You don't have to stand for Christian nation-building to appreciate Prince's artistic attempt and aspiration for redemptive integration of his old music into the new.

Understanding that people are standing up from the dead to build a new nation with Jesus as their leader, Prince moves into inspiration from Proverbs 31 about the role of wives to their husbands. The best of wives wear purple, work with their hands, and are totally devoted to the children and the household. These parts of the album may not find favor with feminists, even some Christian feminists. As a gospel album, it is inspired by other biblical passages. In the book of 2 Samuel 14, we learn the message of Prince's hope—God doesn't kill but creates ways for "banished ones" to return to God if the banished ones are willing to do what they have to do. What is the work? To be the truth. How? One way is to ostracize the ruling class, a common theme in Prince's earlier works, and not interfere with God's apocalypse. Of course, not everyone will do the work, so in one song, Prince writes that a celebration should occur because the banished ones are banished forever. No forgiveness. No compassion. No opportunity for redemption. Yet, it seems that eternal banishment rubs against Prince's tendency toward compassion for the Dearly Beloveds.

Once the Rainbow Children are ready to do the work, they will feel the evangelistic zeal that comes with knowing that they will live eternally in paradise. We must remember that through all this evangelistic Christian nation-building, this is an album written by Prince. The pre-baptized Prince makes appearances—getting undressed, masturbation, and *Kama Sutra* coitus are still available on the Rainbow Children song. Once this is experienced, the woman in the song falls into a state of everlasting sensuality where she is reminded of a "theocratic order" because she is a banished one on the way to reconciliation, if she doesn't flee again. In Prince's pre-baptized stage, there is a small possibility for redemption if you quickly get back to the work after backsliding. She is the wise one's muse who becomes queen to the pharaoh. Is the queen a muse to the pharaoh like a man being married to the purple-clad householding woman who's so good in bed that she can even take over her man's mother's household? This is Prince, the kinky and anti-racist artist who attempts to elevate the consciousness of one's self and does a satisfactory job of it in his song "Family Name," which clearly proclaims racism as a sin. This song ends with a passage from Rev. Dr. Martin Luther King's "I Have a Dream" speech, but given its placement in the song, I don't know if Prince is conveying sarcasm as in, nice speech, but we ain't never going to be free from this. Or, is freedom achieved through hand-holding across our racial differences singing "free at last" the way to everlasting paradise?

I think the answers to my questions lie in the following song, "The Everlasting Now." It is seemingly a tribute to King, where Prince writes that a "brother," presumably a Black man, taught a racially integrated society how to "sing," leading to changing the flag's colors (presumably representing the red, white (supremacy), and blue of the US flag), yet the brother will still be known by a racial slur. The good news? There is life everlasting, regardless—even if only for a few. This song is an ecstatic celebration of the Christian promise, perfect for some sacred dance moves.

The Rainbow Children is also very problematic. Are there hints of antisemitism? Each time I listened to "Muse 2 the Pharaoh," I was repeatedly jarred by his reference to the Holocaust as well as the Jewish names in "Family Name." When I contemplate "banished ones," I cannot help but wonder, based on old Seventh-day Adventist world and cosmic views: are the banished ones Jews, Catholics, and Universalists? If so, these references spoil the album for me, theologically and ethically.

***

The Rainbow Children is an album about redemption in the lives of those who were saved for the Second Coming of Jesus, to be ruled by him and God, and to live in paradise forever. The album ends with a profound invitation to reflect on the final days of one's life and to ask oneself how one lived their life. He asks, "Did you feel redeemed?" and continues the songs with possible flashpoints and touchstones to inspire contemplation, motivation, recommitment, and action. But that sheen of patriarchy and hatred lingers.

Looking for Redemption

One song that I feel is redemptive when paired with his earlier recordings is "$" on *LOtUSFLOW3R*, released in 2009 when Prince was in his early fifties. In "$," he wrote about a popular woman and a man attracted to her, meeting at a bar. She notices and approaches him. It's a meaningless financial transaction—she wants the money, he wants the attention, and it means nothing more. She's not going to love him, he is not going to become the man he wants to be because she wants the money, he's willing to give it, and when they're in the sex act, he can imagine she is someone who adores him. Prince sings that even all the money in the world can't buy the love he is seeking, and physical money really has no intrinsic value. This song is redemptive when paired with songs about using women or believing that using women will result in a healthy relationship.

Overcoming delusion to know God and true joy and what God and true joy are not—money and sex—is what Prince was singing about in his fifties, but in his teens and twenties, sex was the ultimate experience—no matter the motivations. His cosmic evolution is also expressed in "Boom," where he wrote about other worlds, our consciousness expanding beyond "this dirty room." Is the dirty room the violent room of "The Ballad of Dorothy Parker"? I think the dirty room is a deluded mind, not The Great Controversy conflicted consciousness that arose when Prince was in the bathtub, taking his pants off and putting them back on. The dirty room is our ignorance of how things, including ourselves, really are. Prince still believed in the apocalyptic destruction of human beings, but what if we could open our minds, with each other, to a more spatial awareness? A nondual awareness that doesn't need a crucible of temptation, a priest and an angel to manifest an understanding of what reality is? Is the boom in "Boom" the new vehicle to everlasting life? In Prince's religious traditions, the true believers were saved from destruction in the past and will be saved in the future. What will the new "1999" look like and when will it be? Maybe we should enjoy our lives more, but without the futility of "D.M.S.R." and "Let's Go Crazy/ Let's Get Nuts."

What was limiting Prince's dream-interpreter, parable-writer, spiritual evolutionary expression? I have a hypothesis. Prince struggled for years between meeting the kinky demands of his adoring public and his need to provide them spiritual upliftment. This tension persisted throughout his nearly forty-year recording career. During these years, he matured through the normal life cycles and intentional spiritual work, but much of his art created when he was younger was a sort of replication of his younger mindset—the *Sex in the City* Conundrum, I referenced earlier in the book. Now, I'd like to explain it more.

Sex in the City, the television series, premiered in 1998 and ended in 2004. Two movies followed in 2008 and 2010 and a sequel television series in 2021. In my view, the younger, sexy, fun-loving, and mostly free-wheeling yet anxious women friends who were on the prowl and trying to figure out whether marriage was the key to happiness in 1998 (and I loved the show for that) were still on the prowl in 2008, 2010, and to a large degree in 2021, nearly twenty years later when real women would be nearing or experiencing menopause and perhaps changes in their sex drives. Though there had been marriages, affairs, new pairings, being widowed, coming out, etc., their characters' prowling behavior was largely stuck in a youthful consciousness and active libido that made the original series popular, but left the characters portrayed as anachronistic—stuck in a past era, because they, in their near senior citizen years, were still seeking external validation while trying to strut in shoes too narrow for their aging feet. Well, I'm exaggerating, but you dig the picture, right?

Some of Prince's lyrics in his fifties, at the end of his recording career, leave me feeling like he was stuck, mostly singing about his own version of *Sex in the City*, but not because that was his deepest desire but because he wanted to please his fans who had come to expect the sexual consciousness of the young buck Prince, who like the *Sex in the City* characters, was trying to strut gracefully in high heels with old feet.

In 2009, Prince, in his fifties, released *LOtUSFLOW3R*. In this album I found what I had been searching for! Right there in "Colonized Mind," the emancipatory lyrics I sought from him when he was younger. (I will admit again that there is no way I could know or will know all of Prince's music because it is rumored that there are hundreds of songs yet to be recorded and released.) In "Colonized Mind," Prince writes about uploading and downloading into a collective consciousness, karma as in cause and effect, and what causes us to lose our liberated minds: the notion of a master race, a vision of disconnected people, the binary of a two-party political system that appears to offer real choice, and the ongoing colonizing history of these consciousness-limiting phenomena.

How does one rectify the images, the lyrics, the kinky, objectifying, loveless, and sacrilegious artifacts of one's own previously created and still currently available art when the artist has changed? Can we appreciate Prince's redemptive efforts even if those attempts go unnoticed and if unnoticed, as if it is in the water we drink, should that be held against or for the artist? To see if it is possible to redeem one's self, one's art, let's take a peek into Prince's last three albums (that I know of) recorded and released before he died.

In *ART OFFICIAL AGE* (2014) the album, he implored in "Art Official Cage" for free people to liberate others and in "affirmation I & II" about the ways words, especially possessive words like "me" and "mine," are used to keep us apart. In "affirmation III," a sequel, Prince states that it was a delusion to see one's self as separate from others—we are everything we can imagine. Prince, in his fifties, was still concerned about freedom and liberation. I think he became more sophisticated, if you will, about his understanding and expression of nondual consciousness. In *HITNRUN Phase One* (2015) and *HITnRUN Phase Two* (2015), it appears that the *Sex in the City* Conundrum that wasn't present on his 2009 *LOtUSFLOW3R* boomeranged six years later to give a certain fandom what they had always been given, even though many in this certain segment of his fandom had aged beyond menopause, penile dysfunction, and everything else that changes hormonally as we age. Prince, who was once very concerned with correctly telling end times was producing lyrics anachronistic with his own "here today" lived experience. In short, he wasn't really writing for the old set (his fans from the alpha to the omega, if you will) getting closer to their particular end days. I wonder if he was busy preparing for his own final days. I cannot imagine he wasn't doing some of that life review work given how much he implored his fans to get ready to live in paradise forever, or die brutally.

Practice

Renouncing Scapegoating

It seems to me that much conflict and war is based on our present-day understanding of history—not our lived experience of people unless we are living or lived in a war zone. Yet, we wage and fight wars against others based on things people did hundreds and thousands of years ago. We hurt, even kill, innocent people based on what people we don't know, living in other countries, do to others. Oftentimes, we don't trust our own lived experiences of the goodness and neighborliness of those who live nearby. It breaks my heart.

Refer back to chapter five where we discussed creating a genogram. Creating a thorough genogram may reveal how violence and hatred impacted your family. Maybe by focusing on the intergenerational transmission of beliefs about people who do not belong to your religion or ways of identification, you can see how your perception of others may have been influenced by what familial authority figures said. How did they blame people for their own misery? How did they come to categorize a group of people as innately sinful, worthy of punishment, banishment, ostracization, or extermination? What warnings did they give you about "those people"? What are the superstitions we carry? What gets in the way of us taking responsibility for our own dissatisfactions, failures, and disappointments? The answers to the questions may not come quickly or easily, so take some time to allow them to emerge. When they do, make a vow to refrain from blaming people for something, anything, just because they belong to a group you do not belong to. When you make that decision to renounce scapegoating, you can turn your attention back to yourself to examine your thoughts and behaviors and hold yourself accountable and responsible for your life.

8
Conclusion

Dearly Beloved,

Did you wait for it? By now, if you've read this book, engaged in the invitations to reflect on your innate goodness, experimented with the spiritual practices, and contemplated your religious and spiritual inheritance and history, then perhaps you may be more in touch with your belovedness than you were when you began reading this book. I truly hope so. If not, there is no need to negatively judge yourself or conversely inflate your ego. I just wanted to take one more opportunity in this last chapter to encourage you to slow down and remember to take time now and then to experience your goodness, tenderness, vulnerability, and preciousness. In doing so, you may be reminded of your free will, the liberty of consciousness so central to Prince's beliefs and life, so that when you recognize that freedom in the context of the reality of your existential situation and our collective existential threat—climate catastrophe—you will make ethical decisions accordingly.

I believe Prince was a phenomenal worldwide and enduring success not just because he was multi-talented, prodigious, rebellious, and exceptionally entertaining (and gorgeous) but because he was committed to making people feel loved through art, performance, and his deep compassion for the salvation of others. He was a preacher in the boudoir of life and had a stealthy pastoral power. Being gathered together, as he called us to do through music, was a method whereby we could enjoy his music and one another as he expediently professed his religious beliefs through funk, rock, and R&B. The message obviously was not consistently delivered convincingly or forthrightly. For Prince to remain free to define himself as an artist beyond the narrow categories of Black, R&B, funk, rock, or pop, he had to ensure that his gatherings included all races and ethnicities, all conventional and "queer" appearing people, who would be exposed to a feminized Black heterosexual man with racial and gender-diverse bands playing salacious funk, rock, pop, and R&B gospel. I hope I made the case that Prince was a gospel artist.

Prince was an imperfect and evolving anti-Black racism performer and thus activist. The body of his work, from beginning to end, busted culturally limiting myths about what "Black music" should be. His artistic collaborators portrayed racial inclusivity. His public contractual disputes led him to become "The Artist Formerly Known as Prince," and therefore a Black liberated artist and art liberationist. His song "Baltimore" let his fans know he was on the side of unarmed Black men. In "Family Name," he was sure to let his Black listeners know that the words "Black" and "white" to describe people are a "fallacy." Being gathered with and through Prince meant one would very likely be taken outside their comfort zones of similarity, familiarity, Black racial objectification, and racial justice. My white evangelical college friend Debbie (with the scantily clad Prince poster in her dorm room) and I were dissimilar in many ways, even though we were raised in Christian reformist traditions, but with Prince, we found our ground of cross-cultural appreciation. Tens of thousands if not hundreds of others throughout the country were probably experiencing something similar in the late 1970s and early 1980 as Prince was emerging from Minneapolis to the world.

To be recognized as vulnerable to suffering while also precious, in Prince's belief system—Seventh-day Adventism, God's wrath, judgment, and annihilation coming soon— there was a consistent immediacy to Prince's message to repent for possible redemption. But the pursuit and glorification of sexual pleasure with whomever, wherever, disrupted his ministry because it was not understood, especially in the first decades of his career even though there was evidence of his growing spirituality, his commitment to love, that was becoming more manifest in his songs and in the movie

Graffiti Bridge. However, by this time, he had conditioned his fans, now worldwide, to interpret his art from the perspective of a sex machine, not a revealer of religious and spiritual truths and existential concerns unless we had been conditioned by our religious and spiritual traditions to hear it; if we had, this may explain why Prince, the religious sex machine, was controversial, misunderstood, demonized, targeted, and rated "E" by the PMRC as explicit. Time and familial responsibilities have helped me understand the warning.

As a parent who began raising a child (we adopted her when she was seven years old) in the middle of Prince's recording career, I can't say that I wanted her to listen to Prince. I introduced her to Anita Baker and Bob Marley and The Wailers, for example. She also loved Karen Clark Sheard, Elvis Presley, and Rascal Flatts. I was proud that my child had an appreciation for all kinds of music. I remember one day playing the *Chicago* soundtrack because I wanted to choose a theme song we could bond to. I chose "I Can't Do It Alone." I felt confident that when we danced, sang, and acted together to and with the song, she would begin to sense that I was trying to build trust, support, co-creative collaboration, and fun! My partner participated in all of it. I wanted us to be family to one another by making an attempt to include sharing cultural artifacts. Sometimes, we'd act out the dancing part where Velma Kelly (who killed her sister and husband, but my child didn't know this part of the story) performs before Roxie Hart (who killed her lover, and again, my child didn't know this part of the story) to get Roxie to replace Velma's sister in their vaudeville act. Roxie isn't impressed, so Velma wows Roxie with one last act singing, "But I simply cannot do it alone." This is just one way we invited our child to be a part of us. As she grew older and listened to the whole album, and as I lost cognizance of her developing curiosity, we played the album many times before she asked a question about what something in another song meant. In the song "Cell Block Tango," Velma sings that she caught her sister and her husband doing the "spread eagle." Our daughter asked, "Mommy, what is the spread eagle?" Like Velma, well I was in a state of shock because I was caught off guard. I was not ready to share information about oral sex, infidelity, betrayal, and murder with my young daughter. I share this story to say that warning labels can help us guide and teach our children, but the impetus behind labeling can be expressed in censorship. Prince's music, I argue, was not intended for children, but children, even with warning labels, will hear the music and then grow into their own interpretations of what his music means. Parents, pay attention to what your young children are consuming.

As Prince matured, his body of work showed more complexity—from satiating carnal desires through objectifying himself and others to knowing love and incorporating love into animal desire leading to the character development and projections of women with feelings and agency. His album and movie, *Graffiti Bridge*, are pieces of art about being Dearly Beloved, gathering together in different ways in a neighborhood representing the world, each gathering for their own distorted purposes doing their own narcissistic, greedy, and nasty thing, and needing an angel as an intercessor to help flawed human beings turn against greed and toward collaboration and God. According to *Graffiti Bridge*, we need to try to get across the bridge from sinfulness to everlasting life, together across our differences. The bridge is not of one ethnic or racial or cultural tradition—it is the best manifestation of us being Dearly Beloved gathering together to survive Armageddon. The multicolored bridge with wise words tagged onto it is a pathway to get through this thing, this mystery that we call life, but even in calling it such, "life," it is still a mystery, in part because we've yet to experience the afterworld.

Life *is* mysterious. This is an important fact from the religious and spiritual perspectives of Prince. We have no ability to know everything about this thing, which is confounding, full of riches, poverty, love, violence, immense yet filled with pettiness, a place of birth and death, pain, pleasure, sex, and abstinence from sex. What is a person to do and when are they to do it, especially when The Great Controversy, the good and evil powers that continue to war with one another and humanity, wreaks havoc while we strive to maintain our free will? Can we get through this thing well without faith in God? Do we need to reject the psychological sciences and psychiatric medicine if we have faith? What happens when our faith ends in disappointment, over and over again? Why does the glitter and glam of the pop life also offer addiction, poverty, and ignorance? Why is there so much governmental corruption in the United States, the country that inherited the Christian reformist tradition, is informed by the tradition, and espouses liberty of conscience codified in the First Amendment of the US Constitution, but needs adherence to the Fourteenth Amendment to make liberty of conscience available to all? Getting through this thing is a hardship for many, but Prince believed it is made easier when controversies, great and small, can be reconciled toward God to prevent being irretrievably damaged in the apocalypse.

***

I believe his art inspires spiritual practices that have been included throughout this book. The purposes of these practices are to recognize our Dearly Beloved nature and to support us in getting through this thing called life. What is life? According to Prince, there is God's creation, human beings in the Garden of Eden, evil, temptation and succumbing to it, sex, conception, birth, competition, devotion and disdain, death, growth, sexual urges, pleasure-seeking, pain avoidance, discrimination, convention, despair, hope, art, censorship, different belief systems, marriage, divorce, mental illness, spiritual fitness, wealth, poverty, creativity, capitalism, exploitation, rebellion, love, hatred, ignorance, fear, free will, stupidity, drugs, addiction, abuses of all kinds, war and weapons of mass destruction, grief, and the opportunity, in this life, here and now, to avoid an afterlife of suffering. Consequently, from Prince's point of view, we refuse to take this opportunity seriously. So, in life, there is also pity, judgment, compassion, and the ingredients for making a mission. Certainly, there is more to life than this, much more. From atoms to stars, from one's residence to the galaxies, from a watchtower to determine that time is beyond the instruments we have to measure it with certainty, life is beyond our comprehension.

Being humble in the face of scientific discoveries and the proliferation of artificial intelligence means that understanding this thing, called life, is its own conundrum, and as such, some of us will seek clarity and hold fast to what we think is the clear truth of this thing we call life. How will evil and temptation impact our ability to live as well as possible?

The Great Controversy, conceptually, has existed since the creation of consciousness. No matter how long, the nature of being human means as we grow, if we're fortunate, we learn along the way about the thoughts and behaviors that can lead to self-and-other-inflicting wounds. We learn that giving in to our every temptation negatively impacts our personality development and diminishes our capacity for trusting relationships. Depending on one's religious and spiritual beliefs, giving in to temptation is caused by an evil entity—Prince called it Satan, Spooky Electric, the de-elevator, and troubled winds. From another perspective, in particular, the *Kama Sutra*, having sexual urges is not innately evil; on the contrary, they can be made more heavenly the more it is one's intention to be sexually pleasing, not exploitative. This thing called life offers contradicting beliefs as well as resources for resolving some of the minor contradictions, but The Great Controversy will be resolved only by God.

Some say we ought not rely solely on our own understanding while other belief systems call for deeply understanding one's lived experience before believing what others say. Prince's body of work is confusing because it incorporates the "vice" of sexual temptation and regularly giving in to it, female sexual objectification, as well as agape love, sobriety, anti-Black racism, and respect for God and his teachings in the Bible as Prince understood them. It is unfortunate that people turn against one another in the name of religion, and Prince revealed, later in his career, that salvation would be on the backs of the banished—a belief I categorically reject.

Prince was humble about his belief that The Great Controversy he based his art on would not be resolved or reconciled by him, no matter how much he crafted his art on the concept. But since evil and temptation would be with us until Judgment Day, it would be a subject of his artistic expression. This life is full of temptations, caused by evil or an inability to control one's impulses, and self-control and renouncing evil are characteristics one should aspire to on the spiritual path.

I, like Prince, grew up with exposure to United Methodist Church teachings. My college friend Debbie grew up in an evangelical church. Prince grew up in the Seventh-day Adventist Church—all Protestant reformist traditions, and all adhering to the belief in an afterworld. These teachings begin very early in a Christian's life. The prayer I was taught as a child was

> Now I lay me down to sleep,
> I pray the Lord my Soul to keep
> If I should die before I wake,
> I pray the Lord my Soul to take

It is said that this prayer first appeared in *The New England Primer*, published for educating children in the US colonies in the late 1600s. Through intergenerational transmission, this prayer got into the United Methodist Church, the Seventh-day Adventist Church, and probably many other churches.

Prince's understanding of the afterworld is divided, as The Great Controversy is divided, between good and evil. His catalog suggests that no matter what we do in our lives, it would still be up to God and his judgment whether we would be part of the afterworld paradise. Nevertheless, while we are here now, gathered or not, humanity runs the risk of experiencing a wrathful Second Coming of Jesus. So, should we just let go of all inhibitions, restraints, conventional medicines, and attempts to survive—go crazy and nuts—in response to the apocalypse, the climate catastrophes right before our eyes? Based on his art, Prince moved past that way of surrender. He took up the way of the Jehovah's Witnesses, asking band members to hand out religious literature at his concerts. This was the man who performed in the 2007 Super Bowl halftime show and chose to sing Bob Dylan's "All Around the Watchtower," inspired, in part by Isaiah 21. We can let it all hang out on Judgment Day, which might be any day, at any time during the day. But before that, we can tell people that the "day" is coming—it's a creeping reality with evidence all around us. How we share the reality of our impending ecological doom, what has been called the Anthropocene, is up to us artists—the ones who know the arts of living well with nature.

As I have reflected on Prince's art for this book, the question keeps arising about whether, as he was maturing in every way, he was intentionally trying to redeem himself. I think he was making attempts, but it appears from his art that it was difficult trying to reconcile the Protestant reformist beliefs about sex with the fact of his sexual nature, the *Kama Sutra*, the powerful backlash of the PMRC, the deformity and death of his child even after fervent prayer, stress in his first marriage, and being mentored into the Jehovah's Witness tradition by bassist Larry Graham. After baptism, it appears he looked back on his art to contemplate the impact of his art on the young people the PMRC was originally concerned with—the new breed generation for sexual freedom turned into the new breed generation to create a Christian nation. Diamonds and pearls were used seductively, then as symbols of love. This 2004 quote still stands out for me:

> When you're a young man, you think you're the center of the universe. Later you see you're just part of it. The world is only going to get harder. Me and my crew, we love having conversations about music, but when we get deep, we talk about the future, about what we're leaving for the kids.

What did Prince leave for the kids? Focusing only on the eighty-three songs referenced in this book, I argue that Prince left a legacy—a funky-rock-R&B-pop-gospel legacy—that acknowledges how difficult it is to become a person of sexual restraint and faith, especially when one is richly rewarded for portraying just the opposite. This legacy might be embraced by beloved recording artists who are here now also trying to help people get through this thing called life but are also creating and proliferating art that diminishes others, then praising God during their acceptance speeches when they receive an award. But the adults Prince wanted to leave something to need not be recording artists, just consumers of his art, taken as a whole.

We can contemplate what art is doing for us and to us. Does it help us see each other as vulnerable, tender, and in need of compassion? Does it help us be gathered in ways where we give and receive our best? Do we better understand how precious it is to be here and that in being here we have countless opportunities to grow up and into our higher selves, even though life is confounding and difficult? Does the art we consume help us to be people of inner contentment, like those in Paisley Park, in a world of strife and evil? Populated by people who strive to knock us down a peg from time to time? Does the art uplift and inspire us to work through the mental and spiritual challenges ahead of us rather than giving in to resignation? I think Prince's body of work does this. That is why, as I said at the beginning of this book, with a career of nearly forty years, a body of work infused with Christianity from beginning to the end, and having sold more than 100,000,000 records before he died, Prince should be inducted into the Gospel Hall of Fame. But even if he is never nominated or accepted, I would love to hear more gospel artists perform and record Prince's music.

When I heard the Charlotte, North Carolina, gospel group Sainted perform "Purple Rain" on the reality show *America's Got Talent*, I experienced what it feels like to be a Dearly Beloved. The first time I saw it, I had goosebumps and I told my friend that the performance was what my book is all about. The second time I saw it, I teared up. When I heard the back story of how Sainted was allowed to perform the song, I realized it may take many resources and connections to get Prince's music performed and recorded. For example, the record and television show producer Simon Cowell, who is also a judge on *America's Got Talent*, said that "Purple Rain" is his favorite song of all time and that Prince was the greatest artist of all time. It was Cowell who engaged in the eleventh-hour negotiation between *America's Got Talent* and Prince's estate to gain the right for Sainted to perform "Purple Rain." Power, access, passion, talent, devotion, and wealth are what allowed the performance to take place. When I heard Sons of Serendip's, also contestants on *America's Got Talent*, "Purple Rain," I felt awash in the sweet baptismal rain of Micah Christian's voice and Mason Morton's harp. My hope is that Prince's estate will enter into more negotiations with various artists, including more gospel artists, even if they don't have a Simon Cowell-like broker to advocate and negotiate on their behalf.

Why license recording rights to others when people can just listen to Prince's recordings? Prince was channeling Creator spirit and re-interpreting sacred teachings that didn't belong to him but to humanity. The transformative power of Prince's music is not just in the past of his performances, lest the dead follow the dead, but in future gospel interpretations of his art for future generations. I proclaim that the time has come for a Prince revival—a gospel-inspired resurrection of his music from the vault tomb for the purposes of liberation. Again, I know this won't be easy not only because of the resources required but also because some of his more overtly sexual pieces remain misunderstood and thus unnecessarily controversial. Still, sex, sexuality, and sexual expression have their place in the revival because Prince dared to address our most powerful and procreative urge—sex—and then spiritually matured by integrating love, then devotion, into that powerful aspect of being human.

In doing so, Prince reminded us—only as a sexy M.F. international lover could: no matter who you are, and no matter who we are, we are the Dearly Beloved.

Epilogue

This Is What It Feels Like When Doves Cry

Listen Along

Watch Prince's 2007 Super Bowl Halftime performance and listen to "When Doves Cry" before reading this dedication.

    Mmrerevverer reererrrrrrrrrrrr
    Thu-du-dda-Dah
    Thu-du-dda-Dah
    Thu-du-dda-Dah
    Thu-du-dda-Dah

Thu-du-dda-Dah
UH!
Yaaah-wel, yaaah-wel, yaaah-wel, yaaah-wel
    So this is what it sounds like—when they cry?

I heard your falsetto
but not the words—virgin ears
my body, too
we were both young and Black
in the '80s
in the White Midwest
in America, America
God shed HIS grace on thee
    funny how the two are conflated
        I was suffocating under the weight of
            all that smug hypocrisy.

Surrounded by stained glassed bloodied Jesus
trying to be goody goody and reformed
U were bucking it all, young buck
being really bad and reforming
by way of your refrains
like the chorus of my church hymns sung by the
    choir
mesmerizing mantras to make me
a believer
    I believed
        When I heard you sing, something told me
            it was time to grow up.

Up on the one
down on the two
over and over U had us hypnotized
kind of like twirling dervishes
out of control in bliss and
dizzy on prurience
by the swish and swing of
sex
salvation
sex
salvation
titillation and
shame
man, that wasn't cool *before* the initiation
but *after* ritual and rite?
Ah, God Kama!
U knew what time it was and I
had no clue, clock, or calendar
U were trying to be
Father Time and The Afrodisiactic Black Man all
    in one or
were you the Prince of Light and the Prince of
    Darkness
Livin' out loud The Great Controversy?
> *Growing pains hurt! I felt the tension of*
> *being divided against myself—body vs.*
> *belief. Thank God you didn't and*
> *couldn't expose me.*

We were giddy up and down
on the seesaw
The Park with us court-children on rides
in our hearts
but in your third eye's prism first
framed by shadowed and mascaraed eyelids
U were the sweet dreamer Park ranger
dressed in your own
technicolor dream coats—never just one—with
   high-heeled boots to match, of course
               You were saying that I could break
               out of those square molds and be
               fabulous. Sho' nuff!

Kaleidoscopic funky beats and
rock guitars to
The Gospels of
Jesus
the books of the
prophets
Prince—of peace and p—y?
Your Excellency of Enigmatica!
were you really someone we could never understand? That may have been your choice
your fault.
               You were a seductive man of mystery,
               but ain't it better sometimes to just
               leave some of that kinky stuff to
               one's imagination?

With that voice so high, sweet, orgasmic
a pretty man-child soundin' like a
woman, hot and wild
wet, flush and mush
to a bop, a purple sex fetish stone on an altar
and that hairy beast in a pocket
like a heat sensing bomb then
a strut
a pimp
a twirl and
a split in those Park ranger high heels
a filthy mind and mouth that spewed
    obscenities—when you could get away with it
an open heart that said, "Beat Me," strapped in
    black leather ready to
beat someone yourself?
        From you I learned something about
                what's worth fighting for.

Kama Sutra had you in a real vice grip
gripping and dripping
cosmic ecstasy
U were trying to embody
The Great Controversy—and you did—but who
    saw it?
        I didn't know you were really trying to work
          out the most intractable issues ever known
          to humankind! I thought you just wanted
          us to have some fun—1999 style.

A revolutionary's zeal to re-reveal
with the third eye's prism
1980s squares squared
demolition on
acid-tripped hippies and
anarchist punks
U had the look and the style
let's party like it's the end of the world or
1844 backmasked
but it wasn't the time
2,300 days
but it wasn't the time
2,300 years
but it wasn't the century
1999–2000 and
sanctification ain't really up to us

> *Why did you keep telling us that time was up when you also said you just wanted to have some fun? You said we shouldn't stress, that there'd be no injury. Bullshit! Getting through this thing called life is no joke!*

U learned U didn't know the time
so learned about
timelessness
and declension going
round and round

down and down
U could be humble in secret, I read
*It's crazy-making trying to know the unknowable,
right? I mean, how can you know what's right
to do and when to do it if all these disasters
make you reprioritize every thing?*

Private masturbation, critics in the Big Apple, red
vroom-vroom, then
your most precious dominatrix who didn't give a
damn where she was, who was watching, or
what she did or with what
with toys to turn a body on, then out
masturbation fascination or just for shock value
U hated boundaries, did U not?, so
U blew the lid of that sucka
the roof off that mutha
then they put a lid on U, and themselves, and us too
land of the free, but not too free, right? America,
America the beautiful
and you were beautiful too
*I wondered whether my belovedness was based on how much
I praised and protected your vulgarity 'cause usually I didn't
say that shit or think all those thoughts out loud.*

The Revolution,
revelation, resolution
warning, warning, warning

Prince, the Pied Piper of grooming children
All the children yell ABSCAM?
everybody scream PMRC! Rated E.
now that's one label U couldn't beat
but that beat went on, goes on

Mmrerevverer reererrrrrrrrrrrr
Thu-du-dda-Dah
Thu-du-dda-Dah
Thu-du-dda-Dah
Thu-du-dda-Dah
Thu-du-dda-Dah
UH!
Yaaah-wel, yaaah-wel, yaaah-wel, yaaah-wel
    So, this is what it sounds like when
        the doves cry?

Boom, boom, boom. Rat a tat tat
the sound of The Great Controversy
out the necks of doves
on top of the old rugged cross
Babylon babble tower
up down, up down, up down up on the one
down on the two
THERE WAS AN IMPLOSION IN THE
    HOUSE!
Shut our mouths? Damn!
New Power Generation
the Old Power Generation had U, them, us

in a trick bag
But trick(ster), U liked tricks, didn't U, trick?
or was it Father Dick? The obelisk in the earth
giving birth under
candied butter-burnt mountains
peaks protruding past marshmallow clouds
God Almighty making refuge for his people
choking your sword into a plow
U were obscene, wanting us all to be in our
    birthday suits
but you never said you were the only M.F. who
    was sexy

> *Sometimes it, all the revolution, new leaders, new power, felt like too much to take on, but you kept it and us pushing. You said to stand up and get organized. Hmm.*

Who was the game on?
U were beaten, didn't really know the rules
lost a fortune or few
rubbing pennies to make a dollar
Boo hoo poor little rich slave!
made U like Marvin
Wanna Holla!
so go 'head
Holla!!!!!

> *I saw you fighting and I wanted to come to your rescue, but I wasn't always sure you were really fighting for us. Were you?*

Epilogue   219

Yours was an expensive lesson, Kid
didn't always run it better than the
mack runs his b——es
Purple Rain to Graffiti Bridge
New Power Re-Generation
ca-Ching, ca-ching, oh how the dollars
    could sing
the "silent" but loaded servant in golden velvet
    chains
Did Harriet show U how to break them cuffs?

Mmrerevverer reererrrrrrrrrrrr
Thu-du-dda-Dah
Thu-du-dda-Dah
Thu-du-dda-Dah
Thu-du-dda-Dah
Thu-du-dda-Dah
UH!
Yaaah-wel, yaaah-wel, yaaah-wel, yaaah-wel
                    So is this also what freedom
                                sounds like?

U transcended your brand with
a new melding
of old wrought symbols
rising a new myth from
ancient forms
Egypt, Africa, rising in the ankh

emancipator, free to free
and see your people through the prism
on an overground taxicab lane
> *I'd never thought that much about capitalism
> and exploitation. You said freedom and power
> is in owning your own shit. Got it!*

Prince to Formerly Known As . . .
Huh?!
the corporate graffiti-grip stains wiped clean
behold the everlasting love—oceans of aubergine
    flowers
fragrant petals of salt and powder
blooming in the sun
symbolic representation transcending even U
woman in man and man in woman
crucified and resurrected—both more than once
the slave is the liberator
the third eye don't blink
the colors brighten
time for a new education, son
yeah, the salvation from the sinner
and the third-eye prism understood—we are one
Trying to resolve
The Great Controversy
Did you do it?
> *I think you died trying, and at that moment,
> I became the dove*

We need new kinds of leadership, strong and
    capable
for
freedom
love
art
love
art
sex, love, art
Am I repeating myself?
yeah, you said there is joy in saying the same
    things over and over again
call and response, mantra, kirtan
religion
faith
sex
Kama Sutra
love
dating
marriage—
your sacrilege in "Head"
your sanctity in "Forever in My Life"
conception
love
baby
love
illness
love

birth
love
death
love
There is joyful wisdom in "love me" repetition,
    until . . .
> *Prince, you were a Dearly Beloved too who*
> *didn't always understand that some things, like*
> *a child's death, are too much to bear.*
> *Too much to bear. Too much.*

Divorce—
how you begin "If I Was Your Girlfriend" with
    Mendelssohn's "Midsummer Night's Dream"
Thoth, Hermes, phallus
trickster!
little nude Black man on
big Winged White Horse
bare ass in a flower
Camille and Spooky Electric
some of us saw all y'all merging and
    emerging through our kaleidoscopic prism
    collective eye
Did you think we wouldn't see you evolving too?
even the almighty phallus proved an illusion
erect one day
limp the next
but that was okay to our emerging generation

    defining ourselves beyond old gender constructs
        and roles
U did it too, OG!
    Thank God I knew I didn't have to prostrate to
    phallusmania to be beloved. How did I know?
        It was instinctual, and apparently you
            knew it too.

Was there no obstacle to your creativity?
no, just life, death, sorrow and succor
unanswered prayers
guilt, blame, shame, grief
bass and baritone in the earthquake at the GCS
promising everlasting paradise
conviction!
The Great Controversy resolution was already
    written, sucka
nothing else to be revealed
no need for new prophets or messiahs
no Daniels and Michaels
SHUT THAT SHIT DOWN PRINCE! DAMN!
down from the cross but
up back the mystic ladder
rung by jagged rung
each a perilous composite of
clay and iron
wobbling in those heels
bloodied and bunioned
ankh on your back—a purple banana too

superego in check
alter egos screwing in and with your mind
destroyed theologies
reconstructed Christologies
your head holes filled with the Holy Book
your heart filled through prayer
looked a bit like *Kama Sutra*
Is the woman really only to be acted on?
        I'm glad you grew up.

Your third-eye prism refracted
faded colors
purple to lavender
red to pink
green to chartreuse
yellow to beige
a drab pastel inner world
like a mind's eye cataract
you began driving us Miss Daiseys
on flat square tires
in a rusted taxicab
on a cobble-stoned sidewalk
as we heard the clickity clank
clickity clank
of your incessant
apocalyptic warnings
backmasked and
backward
     You could be a real pain in the ass!

A slow trip down a mainstream groove
from The Park to Dolphin Stadium
from ice to rain
Prince, the strutting peacock in turquoise and
    orange
a shapeshifting dolphin when U know U should
    have been in navy blue and white
on the colt
I'm from Naptown, baby, and I don't play
at least you wasn't a bear
I thought U liked being on top of white horses
29–17. Bam!
Who was the game on then?
Bears? Hell no.
Colts? Yes, but really, really, for me
It was all about you—still is.
                      You showed us that it is often of vital
                              importance that we be winners in
                                          this short life.

U said that animals assume curious postures
The *Kama Sutra* people do too
hare, elephant, horse, deer, mare,
and bull
a papal bull on fire?
I guess you were the black colt bucking
on the white-winged horse
with a neigh and doves' wail

Mmrerevverer reererrrrrrrrrrrr
Thu-du-dda-Dah
Thu-du-dda-Dah
Thu-du-dda-Dah
Thu-du-dda-Dah
Thu-du-dda-Dah
UH!
Yaaah-wel, yaaah-wel, yaaah-wel, yaaah-wel
   Sounds like doves and Lady Cabdriver in
   orgasmic chorus, and you taught me that
   it's okay to express cosmic and boudoir ecstasy.

Shepherding the wayward sheep
your master sat upon an ass
one of your favorite pastimes?
   No one ever told me that I was entitled
   to expect pleasure. Thank you for that!

and the Kama people assume positions too
lingam and yoni
moving forward
churning
piercing
rubbing
pressing
blow of boar and bull
with a grunt and a sparrow's sport
a wildcat growled but

the big white bunny said something
in the US zoo
to the rebels you told us not to feed and
the hungry ghosts are still prowling in search of
    The Lamb with two horns
as the zombies eat themselves alive
America, America and The Lamb
funny how the two are conflated
    You tried to save us from getting it twisted, but . . .

The fans. The NY critics. The world. The censors.
U gave us the best of yourselves with
the best of genres
all Along the Watchtower—you kept a view
Bob Dylan
Jimi Hendrix
Foo Fighters
Tina Turner
thank you!
a live phallic festival—the shadow of your guitar
cocked
Oh baby, baby, baby, you had the image!
emancipation, free to do what you did
as the lightning parted the dark sky
they partied like it was the beginning of a new
    dawn
        I never saw you as the savior, but as a
        magnificent spiritual friend. Sho' nuff!

That was 2007, and are things better on earth now than in the afterworld?

> The "todayworld" for
> the prism children
> is in Baltimore and Los Angeles
> it exploded in Minneapolis and Louisville
> Did U feel it in the bardo?
> in the "todayworld" now and forever more
> shall we let ourselves lose our minds and our shit
> as the Creeper-Grinning Reaper of the isms tries to take us down?
> antinomian and declension
> I don't think so
> *Deep in my bones I hear you saying it's time for another "slave" rebellion, and I'm here and down for that.*

> We're in the Purple Reign
> underneath a Purple Cloud
> drenched in the Purple Storm
> flying through a Purple Sky on a
> first class trip
> piloted by the global lover
> frolicking near the sun
> above the mercy seat
> in the yellow rideshare
> with the oversexed driver
> the bathing lady in a fruity French cap

in a tub
shaking and soaking her vajayjay noisemaker
trying to arouse her own ecstasy
some public display of the erotic—at times—
    no matter
she still gets that third-eye prism reflection
that you saw behind the dark pyramid shades
glaring signs and symbols
and all U wanted us to see is
what U saw
with the eye—through the Christ-God-
    Kama prism
re-Awakening the New Prism Sibling
    Revolutionary Generation
us colorful and sexy people of profound content-
    ment (sometimes) committed to justice
    (always)
being purified in
the boudoir, the cesspool, the den of iniquity—call
    it what you will, but can't
in the sportscar
on the way to The Park, again
Did U ever make your way back?
before the Creeper-Grinning Reaper of the Gilded
    Yet Empty Pop Life Age
put something in "your nose" and
knocked you out for good—or so we thought
> *Lover, it's better to have known we were*
> *all beloved before your tragic end, lover.*

But the corporate game is still on, baby, always on
U knew that is what wills are for, right?
momentary acquisition
'cause greed don't stop—it's its own AI
the incubator-sepulchre vault was opened
for more songs
like we needed to hold on to what we can't
like we needed more than what you already gave
Damn!
like the stones removed from the tomb
resurrecting the preacher and prophet
not ready to let go of the joy in

Mmrerevverer reererrrrrrrrrrrr
Thu-du-dda-Dah
Thu-du-dda-Dah
Thu-du-dda-Dah
Thu-du-dda-Dah
Thu-du-dda-Dah
UH!
Yaaah-wel, yaaah-wel, yaaah-wel, yaaah-wel
    I'll seek, but know I'll never find, a sound
    like doves crying. No, not ever again.

The screech
then
the heartbeat
on the one and the two
then three and the 4

4 what?
4 the afterworld in the afterword
4 love
always and forever
4 L-O-V-E.

Afterword

If you began reading *Dearly Beloved* not knowing that Prince's body of work, taken as a whole, is inspired by an evangelical Christian zeal, and you believe I made a convincing case of it, then it is likely you will never listen to Prince's music exactly as you did before. Consequently, I would advise you, as a pastoral counselor does, to give yourself permission to grieve the loss of meaning you had for what you thought Prince's music was, as well as grieve what you thought Prince represented, and mourn who you thought he was.

Through this book I tried to make clear that Prince's body of work was not just for a *Kama Sutra*–filled D.M.S.R.

to perpetuate a Pop Life existence while bathing in a vapid Purple Rain chant. Ultimately his art—taken as a whole—was for inspiring his fans to resolve their shame about their sexual nature as he implored them, us, to climb up The Ladder to avoid de-elevator, as Prince put it. He wanted to channel the love of Christ while giving prophetic voice to the oncoming onslaught of Armageddon where he believed most of us, his and Jesus's beloveds, would die gruesomely. Did Prince's ardent prayers for us require him to be a saint? One need not be a saint to proclaim the need for love and protection, but sometimes, as Prince did, our idols step into and use religious, ancient, and mythical archetypes in their art. In turn, we project saintliness onto them, and in time they begin to identify with those projections, and the feedback loop takes on its own life until it is interrupted by retirement, scandal, or death. Eventually, when their private lives are revealed, we are reminded that they are just like us—imperfect and vulnerable. Until the spell is broken, as long as they are fulfilling our wants and desires for entertainment, and in Prince's case, transcendence, we forget they are fully human. Why?

When it appears as if we are receiving unconditional love, we can be mesmerized by it. I believe the invitation into everlasting life in paradise was an invitation Prince made to all of us, even if that is not what we wanted for ourselves—to strip down and revel in the Holy Spirit. Nevertheless, evangelical zeal, as I understand it, is an emotional-belief system (not exclusive to Christians or religion) whereby true believers like Prince (as I understand his art), are convinced of their rightness. Their excitement about their truth claims doesn't leave much room for another's doubts, disagreements, difference, or distaste. Religious zeal can be simultaneously mesmerizing, contagious, and paradoxically disconcerting when facts challenging the zeal creep into consciousness.

I'll admit that there are times when it is tempting to surrender completely to being mesmerized, falling into contagion or bliss, or a moment of emptiness. You have probably experienced times when your thoughts go round and round the same question or concern, but the circuity of the thought pattern resolves nothing. We call that rumination, and it is very aggravating. Relief from this frustration is necessary to move forward, and relief can be found in a moment of non-discursive mental spaciousness. On the other hand, sometimes the moment of mental freedom can bring such relief that we tend to hang out there, denying the presenting information that contradicts our idol worship. We don't want to cash the reality check we've been given, and refusing to do so has its costs. What do I mean?

While I was writing this book, two noteworthy events happened related to Prince. First, he was posthumously inducted into the Songwriters Hall of Fame! As a fan, I am excited about the long-overdue induction, and I can engage in celebratory contagion about it because I believe Prince was worthy of the honor. I'm truly sorry he wasn't able to receive the award when he was alive. It is regrettable. The second noteworthy event was a news report that a multi-year-long documentary project about Prince's life, not just his art making, might not be released because the producing parties, including the Oscar Award–winning documentarian Ezra Edelman, and Prince's estate could not come to an agreement about what would be an honest account of his life that would also support the flourishing of his legacy and his recording studio playground and home, Paisley Park. Why the concern and tension? The documentary includes an accusation that Prince was physically violent toward one of his girlfriends. This information breaks into the mesmerized consciousness and the celebratory contagion, inviting us to break from our denial and consider more deeply. Accusations of violence are always worthy of consideration, and should we choose to fuel the dissociation through denial, it will come at a cost. What is that cost? The perpetuation of a culture that silences people who are hurt by celebrities as we prop them up as innately incapable of heinousness. Fans would do well to learn how to work through this tension.

Tension, the word and the sensation, seems to fit anything related to Prince's art, and his life as it has been recorded by many authors. The report on the documentary also includes stories about Prince's controlling personality. Many superstars have been described as physically violent, emotionally manipulative, or economically exploitative and controlling behind the scenes. Many superstars. Many. So many that I cannot help but wonder if superstardom itself holds the potential to injure one's personality structure, that is, without consistent grounding in ethical principles by posses who aren't sycophants. Maybe the dynamic works in reserve order. People with injured personality structures use the arts to create a façade of likeability. Maybe there is an alternative trajectory. Perhaps talented yet insecure people create artistic images of superiority to protect themselves from the hurt and grief that will arise when fame dissipates. In any case, what I know for sure from being a pastoral counselor is this: everyone has private and public lives that are not fully integrated and on display all the time. When I say everyone, I mean Prince, too. So what about this fraught tension? Can it be mitigated?

As a Buddhist practitioner, I have learned how to be still with tension, to notice when I'm taking sides in a matter and ask myself "Why?," and to notice when and why my mind goes toward denial, delusion, self-deception, or automatic acceptance. In these moments, I need to remind myself that I am committed to engage in Right Speech so as to refrain from cavalierly passing along hearsay, gossip, or idle speech just to fill the silence. Tension is what we will have to live with as we continue consuming Prince's art as we grow older and face our complexified existential situations. Complexified by what? Everything including birth, illnesses, old age, authoritarianism, international war, civil war, post-truth cultures, nuclear weapons, corporate greed and worker exploitation, old geopolitical grudges, artificial intelligence, genocide, climate catastrophe, deadly illicit drugs, and more. How will we get through this thing called life? It's an enormous existential question because there is so much within life to take us down, so let's break the bigger existential question down into smaller existential questions, especially for young people, for this time in history:

1. How can you value yourself as worthy of love and respect if you do not have a large social media audience?
2. How can you pursue the life of the mind, with higher education, without going into life-long debt and the reality of inflation?
3. How will you resist the temptation to use artificial intelligence as your own creative offering?
4. How might you pursue your healthy vocational passions without succumbing to exploiting yourself for the prurient interests of others because that's where the money is?
5. How will you deal with the reality check that being "liked" online is not anywhere close to being loved in person?
6. What support is out there for teaching you how to collaborate with people in person?
7. How will you learn to identify and befriend trustworthy people when you grew up learning to fear potential school shooters?
8. How will you make the most of being here now the harder it gets to survive natural disasters?

The list goes on. Does Prince's music speak to these issues?

New generations are being introduced to Prince's body of work as originally released, as well as brand new releases.

They are encountering his art as they mature into sexual beings who will also face their end days. They are likely to hear Prince in ways similar to his original audience, but I suspect in largely dissimilar ways. Through R&B, funk, and rock, primarily, they can appreciate those elements in Prince's music, but I'm less certain that the young "nones," the religiously unaffiliated and maybe even religiously averse, will appreciate Prince's Christian evangelical zeal. On the other hand, the "spiritual but not religious" younger generations may find and embrace the enduring liberatory love Prince expressed in his music as the spiritual transcendence they seek for dealing with the existential concerns their parents and ancestors did not have to contend with. My hope, as I say with all wisdom traditions, is that if you find something worthwhile in the offering, use it. Prince, in his imperfect royal badness, offered, offered, and offered for nearly forty years. Certainly there is something within the Prince canon you can use to get through this thing called life.

Acknowledgments

I'm grateful to my parents, Virginia and Curtis Pinner, who raised me with an appreciation for African American pop and gospel cultures. Had they not, I would not have encountered Prince's earliest recordings on WTLC in Indianapolis, Indiana, in the late 1970s.

My partner, Tracey Scott, somehow manages to support me, and endure, my projects that sometimes seem to come out of nowhere and disrupt the peace of our lives.

I'm grateful to the former presidents of United Theological Seminary of the Twin Cities, Drs. Barbara Holmes and Lew Zeidner. Dr. Holmes invited me to apply for a teaching position, and after I was hired, Dr. Zeidner asked me why potential students would choose United over other seminaries, and that is when the Theology of Prince project began to twinkle in our eyes.

The twinkle became an idea that we shared with others at the school, so I'm grateful to United Theological Seminary of the Twin Cities and their students, administrators, and faculty from 2017 to 2018 who enthusiastically supported the idea and made it a project. As a project, we visited Paisley Park, and there would have been no Paisley Park without Prince, its curators, caretakers, and other staff. I've been there three times, and each time was an astonishing adventure.

The Theology of Prince project attracted many fans at the school, throughout the Twin Cities, and the world, so I'm thankful to all who participated in the project and contributed to the *Theology of Prince Journal*. As a consequence of the journal and talking about the work, I met people who I probably would have never known they were Prince fans, like Laura Devenney, whose body and voice vibrated and eyes widened when I said "Prince" and "theology." I was always surprised when people responded this way because I thought my Prince work was done, but then I was reminded that maybe there was more to be done, and that maybe I should pay closer attention to people's interests.

Spiritual teachers Sebene Selassie and Koshin Paley Ellison encouraged me to meet the agent for their books, Anna Geller. Anna convinced me to write a book about Prince's theology (even though I had edited the journal). I became convinced that there might be more I had to say about Prince and his music, but I didn't know what I wanted to say, so I put the idea on a long pause.

One day, while visiting the Twin Cities after I had moved to Chicago, I visited my friend Amy Fister, who worked in development for United and was raising funds for Collegeville Institute (CI). Amy encouraged me to meet CI's executive director, Rev. Dr. Jacqueline Bussie, who invited me to spend some time at CI as a short-term resident scholar. I accepted her invitation. Over the nine days I was there in one of their beautiful apartments looking out at the creek, I wrote the book proposal that led to this book.

Forty years ago, a friend who lived and still lives in Minneapolis told me that I belonged there. As someone bent on living in California, I could not understand how he saw me fitting into one of the coldest places I had heard of. Thirty-two years later, I was living in St. Paul and loving it (when it was warm) until I hated it (when it was cold). Nevertheless, I am grateful for the Twin Cities culture and I have a better understanding, I think, why Prince lived and created his world there.

Living in the Twin Cities, I met wonderful people, three of whom have given me feedback on a portion of this book, Zenzele Isoke, Stacy McClendon, and Emily Youngdhal Wright. I've also received feedback from friends and Prince superfans Miriam Phields and Mary Poole Reese.

After writing the book proposal in Minnesota and returning home, I decided I wanted to share the proposal with a Minnesota-based publisher and reached out to Broadleaf Books, where I met one of their editors, Lisa

Kloskin. Naturally, I'm grateful to Lisa for all the work she put into making my manuscript readable, but I feel I owe her an extra solid. Why? I'll keep that a secret, but know that Lisa knows how to work with a writer who is preoccupied with other matters. I also want to thank my editors Erin Gibbons and Diedre Hammons for their suggestions and direction.

You are reading this book for a reason. I'm grateful for your curiosity and I hope you intend to be open to letting these words inspire you to find skillful and joyful ways to face life's challenges without becoming victimized, turning against others, or scapegoating targeted groups. Thank you for opening these pages.

Last, I have to express appreciation for Prince. I hope that this book illuminates parts of his messages that for one reason or another, he was unable to be transparent, literal, or forthright about.

Notes

Chapter 1: Dearly Beloved

7   *Prince was never a member of the TSA.* Janet Kerschner, email to author, March 21, 2024.
13 *"[Prince] was kneeling and praying to God."* Alan Light, *Let's Go Crazy: Prince and the Making of Purple Rain* (New York: Atria Books, 2014), 101.
13 *"Prince was writing songs that were not confused."* Light, *Let's Go Crazy*, 101.
30 *The ankh symbol, which after being redesigned, became Prince's "name."* Margaret Rhodes, "The Fascinating Origin Story of Prince's Iconic Symbol," *Wired*, April 22, 2016, https://www.wired.com/2016/04/designers-came-princes-love-symbol-one-night/.

30   *The ankh is the Egyptian symbol for life, universe, and humanity.* Carl G. Jung, "Approaching the Unconscious," in *Man and His Symbols*, ed. Carl G. Jung and Marie-Luise von Franz (New York: Doubleday Windfall, 1964), 55.
30   *Prince used it in a more stylized form in the movie* **Purple Rain.** Rhodes, "The Fascinating Origin Story of Prince's Iconic Symbol."
44   *"The art of speaking by changing the form of words."* Vatsyayana, *Kama Sutra Complete*, trans. Richard Burton, Bhagavanlal Indrajit, Shivaram Parashuram Bhide, chapter three, part one.
48   *"The great prince who stands watch over the sons of your people."* Vatsyayana, *Kama Sutra Complete*, 1157–8.
50   *"Seventh-day Adventists remained rather consistent."* David Frank Holland, email to author, April 8–9, 2024.

Chapter 2: We Are Gathered

74   ***Build Up is an organization of international activists.*** "About Build Up," Build Up, accessed February 7, 2024, https://howtobuildup.org/about-build-up.
75   *"Worthy are the disinherited."* Pamela Ayo Yetunde, *Vigil: Spiritual Reflections on Your Money and Sanity* (Marabella Books: Avondale Estates, 2011), dedication page.

Chapter 4: To Get Through This Thing

117   *His parents were strict devout Seventh-day Adventists.* Ben Greenman, *Dig If You Will the Picture: Funk, Sex, God and Genius in the Music of Prince* (New York: Henry & Holt), 121.
117   *"Our first big break was."* Mobeen Azhar, *Prince: Chapter and Verse—A Life in Photographs* (New York: Sterling, 2016), 19.
118   *"'We gathered in his dressing room to pray.'"* Mayte Garcia, *The Most Beautiful: My Life with Prince* (New York: Hachette Books, 2017), 124–25.

118 *"Prince changed lyrics on previously released songs."* Alex Hahn, *Possessed: The Rise and Fall of Prince* (New York: Billboard Books, 2003), 221.
118 *"[Prince] sent me one of his new releases in the mail."* Azhar, *Prince: Chapter and Verse*, 94.
119 *He "shape-shifted into this completely different person."* Alan Light, *Let's Go Crazy: Prince and the Making of Purple Rain* (New York: Atria Books, 2014), 266.
119 *"From the perspective of NPG keyboardist Tommy Barbarella."* Hahn, *Possessed*, 227. This song, "Good Pussy," was never released. It can be found on PrinceVault, https://princevault.com/index.php?title=Good_Pussy.
121 *"[W]henever I mentioned Akhenaten and Nefertiti."* Garcia, *The Most Beautiful*, 244.
121 *Graham mostly replaced Garcia.* Hahn, *Possessed*, 221.
121 *"He was hardcore into it."* Garcia, *The Most Beautiful*, 250.

Chapter 5: Called Life

133 *The soul is born into the "same cycle."* Mayte Garcia, *The Most Beautiful: My Life with Prince* (New York: Hachette Books, 2017), 138–139.
133 *Prince shared he believed in reincarnation.* Ben Greenman, *Dig If You Will the Picture: Funk, Sex, God and Genius in the Music of Prince* (New York: Henry & Holt), 117.
133 *"What we say about the situation is very important."* Greenman, *Dig If You Will the Picture*, 118.
139 *Prince is pointing to the intergenerational "legacy burdens."* Richard Schwartz, *No Bad Parts: Healing Trauma and Restoring Wholeness with the Internal Family Systems Model* (Boulder: Sounds True, 2021), 19.
140 *"But the fruit of the Spirit is love."* *The Thompson Chain-Reference Study Bible*, New King James Version, ed. Frank Charles Thompson. (Indianapolis: B.B. Kirkbrige Bible, 1997), 1514.
144 *I decided to continue my research.* Pamela Ayo Yetunde, *Object Relations, Buddhism, and Relationality in Womanist Practical Theology* (New York: Palgrave Macmillan, 2018), 50–51.

Chapter 6: Evil, Temptation, the Afterworld, and Going Crazy

148 *This belief is known as premillennialism.* Touré, *I Would Die 4 U* (New York: Atria Books, 2019), 141.
152 *"When you're a young man, you think."* Alan Light, *Let's Go Crazy: Prince and the Making of Purple Rain* (New York: Atria Books, 2014), 276.
153 *"Prince would never mess around with the devil."* Light, *Let's Go Crazy*, 100.
154 *"And if you're evil I'll forgive you by and by."* Prince and the Revolution, "I Would Die 4 U," track 4 on *Purple Rain,* Warner Bros. Records, 1984.
155 *"'Cause you, I would die for you, yeah."* Prince and the Revolution, "I Would Die 4 U."
157 *Following the chronology of Ireland's seventeenth-century archbishop of Armagh.* Ben Greenman, *Dig If You Will the Picture: Funk, Sex, God and Genius in the Music of Prince* (New York: Henry & Holt), 124.
157 *"Prince occasionally slips into wanting you to think of him as Jesus like."* Touré, *I Would Die 4 U* (New York: Atria Books, 2019), 109.
158 *"'We were sent to help people see.'"* Touré, 112–113.
158 *"'[Prince] had a sense of being called.'"* Touré, 113.
158 *A plan for a tour documentary called* The Second Coming. Greenman, *Dig If You Will the Picture*, 28.
158 *The Second Coming concept had morphed.* Jason Draper, *Prince: Chaos, Disorder, and Revolution* (New York: Backbeat Books, 2011), 89.
159 *457 BCE was the time when the countdown.* E. G. White, *The Great Controversy* (Minneapolis: Remnant Publications, 2001), 173.
160 *"Although the first human couple disobeyed God."* Watch Tower Bible and Tract Society of Pennsylvania, *You Can Live Forever in Paradise on Earth* (New York: Watchtower Bible and Tract Society of New York, 1982), 9.
162 *Prince writes a sermon for the beloved ones.* Prince and the Revolution, "Let's Go Crazy," track 1 on *Purple Rain,* Warner Bros. Records, 1984.

163 *Prince told the comedian Chris Rock.* Light, *Let's Go Crazy*, 99.
163 *It is a sad and tragic irony that Prince died of an opioid overdose.* Kory Grow, "Prince's Cause of Death: Opioid Overdose," *Rolling Stone*, June 2, 2016, https://rol.st/2vj8Xds.
163 *Opioids killed more people in the United States in 2017.* German Lopez, "In One Year, Drug Overdoses Killed More Americans Than the Entire Vietnam War Did," *Vox*, June 8, 2017, https://www.vox.com/policy-and-politics/2017/6/6/15743986/opioid-epidemic-overdose-deaths-2016.
167 *There are many examples that encourage dance.* Alisha Tatem Wimbush, "Dancing Before the Prince of Peace to the Sound of Prince: Working Toward the Integration of Spirituality and Sexuality within a Worshipping Community," *Theology of Prince Journal*, United Theological Seminary of the Twin Cities, 2018–2019, 296.

Chapter 7: Redemption and the Rising of the Rainbow Children

185 *"It isn't expedience, it isn't desperation."* Arion Berger, "The Rainbow Children," *Rolling Stone,* January 2, 2002, https://www.rollingstone.com/music/music-album-reviews/the-rainbow-children-251311.
186 *"The Rainbow Children remains a deliberately confronting album."* Andy Healy, "Prince's The Rainbow Children Turns 20, An Anniversary Retrospective," *Albumism*, November 19, 2021, https://albumism.com/features/prince-the-rainbow-children-turns-20-anniversary-retrospective.

Chapter 8: Conclusion

207 *"When you're a young man, you think you're the center of the universe."* Alan Light, *Let's Go Crazy: Prince and the Making of Purple Rain* (New York: Atria Books, 2014), 276.

Books by Pamela Ayo Yetunde

Songbird Birdsong: The Story (Marabella StoryCraft, 2024)

Casting Indra's Net: Fostering Spiritual Kinship and Community (Shambhala Publications, 2023)

Black and Buddhist: What Buddhism Can Teach Us About Race, Resilience, Transformation, and Freedom, co-edited with Cheryl A. Giles (Shambhala Publications, 2020)

Buddhist-Christian Dialogue, U.S. Law, and Womanist Theology for Transgender Spiritual Care (Palgrave Macmillan, 2020)

Object Relations, Buddhism, and Relationality in Womanist Practical Theology (Palgrave Macmillan, 2018)

Vigil: Spiritual Reflections on Your Money and Sanity (Marabella Books, 2011)

The Inheritance: A Stock-Picking Story (Marabella Books, 2000)

Beyond 40 Acres and Another Pair of Shoes: For Smart Sisters Who Think Too Much and Do Too Little About Their Money (Marabella Books, 1998)